Table of Contents

Batter Up!	3
Beginning Consonants: b, c, d, f, g, h, j	4
Beginning Consonants: k, l, m, n, p, q, r	5
Beginning Consonants: s, t, v, w, x, y, z	6
Ending Consonants: b, d, f, g	7
Ending Consonants: k, l, m, n, p, r	8
Ending Consonants: s, t, x	9
Blends: fl, br, pl, sk, sn	10
Nothing But Net	11
Consonant Digraph th	12
Read and Write Digraphs	13
Ending Digraphs	14
Missing Digraphs	15
Silent Letters	16
Sounds of c and g	17
Hard and soft c and g	18
Short Vowel Scrapbook	19
Short Vowel Scrapbook	20
Kick It In!	21
Long Vowels	22
Super Silent e	23
Review	24
Missing Vowel Pairs	25
Missing Vowel Pairs	26
Y as a Vowel	27
Compound Your Effort	28
Mixing a Compound	29
Prefix re	30
Prefixes un and dis	31
Suffixes ful, less, ness, ly	32
Suffixes and Meanings	33
Suffixes er and est	34
Scale the Synonym Slope	35
We Go Together!	36
Amazing Antonyms	37
Trading Places	38
Antonym or Synonym?	39
Contractions	40
Something Is Missing	41
Common Nouns	42
Proper Nouns	43

Singular Nouns 44
Plural Nouns 45
Action Verbs 46
Better Sentences 47
Kinds of Sentences 48
Four Kinds of Sentences 49
My Bag's Ready! 50
Slam Dunk! 51
Clue Caper! 52
Make the Touchdown! 53
Game Story 54
Story Sequence 55
Same/Different: Venn Diagram 56
Same/Different: Ann and Lee Have Fun 57
Classifying 58
Birds 59
Cathy Uses Context Clues 60
Cathy Uses More Context Clues 61
Comprehension: Ladybugs 62
The Statue of Liberty 63
Main Idea 64
What Doesn't Belong? 65
What Will They Do? 66
How Will It End? 67
Clues to Conclusions 68
Extra! Extra! Read All About It! 69
Answer Key 70–80

School Specialty Publishing

Copyright © 2006 School Specialty Publishing. Published by Brighter Child®, an imprint of School Specialty Publishing, a member of the School Specialty Family.

Printed in the United States of America. All rights reserved. Except as permitted under the United States Copyright Act, no part of this publication may be reproduced or distributed in any form or by any means, or stored in a database or retrieval system, without prior written permission from the publisher, unless otherwise indicated.

Send all inquiries to:
School Specialty Publishing
8720 Orion Place
Columbus, OH 43240-2111

ISBN 0-7696-7672-3

2 3 4 5 6 7 8 9 10 WAL 09 08 07

Name _____

Batter Up!

What did Bobby yell to the batter?

Directions: To find out, say the name of each picture. On the line, write the letter that you hear at the beginning of each picture.

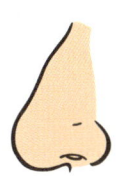

©2006 School Specialty Publishing   3   Reading: Grade 2

Name _____

Beginning Consonants: b, c, d, f, g, h, j

Directions: Fill in the beginning consonant for each word.

Example: __c__ at

____ox

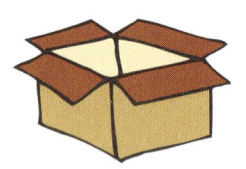

____acket

____oat

____ouse

____og

____ire

Reading: Grade 2   ©2006 School Specialty Publishing

Name _____

Beginning Consonants: k, l, m, n, p, q, r

Directions: Write the letter that makes the beginning sound for each picture.

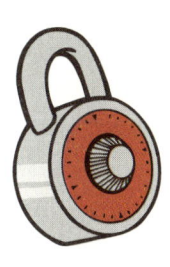

©2006 School Specialty Publishing   5   Reading: Grade 2

Name _____

Beginning Consonants: s, t, v, w, x, y, z

Directions: Write the letter under each picture that makes the beginning sound.

Reading: Grade 2   6   ©2006 School Specialty Publishing

Name _____

Ending Consonants: b, d, f, g

Directions: Fill in the ending consonant for each word.

ma ____

cu ____

roo ____

do ____

be ____

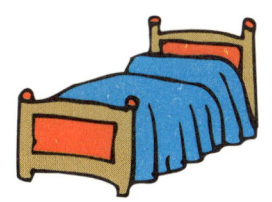

bi ____

Ending Consonants: k, l, m, n, p, r

Directions: Fill in the ending consonant for each word.

nai ____

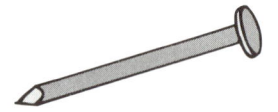

ca ____

gu ____

ca ____

truc ____

ca ____

pai ____

Name _____

Ending Consonants: s, t, x

Directions: Fill in the ending consonant for each word.

ca ____

bo ____

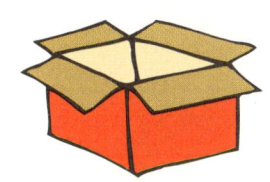

bu ____

fo ____

boa ____

ma ____

Name _____

Blends: fl, br, pl, sk, sn

Blends are two consonants put together to form a single sound.

Directions: Look at the pictures and say their names. Write the letters for the beginning sound in each word.

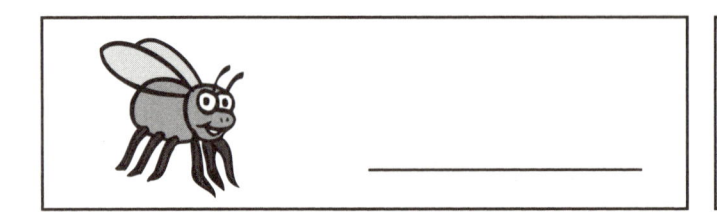

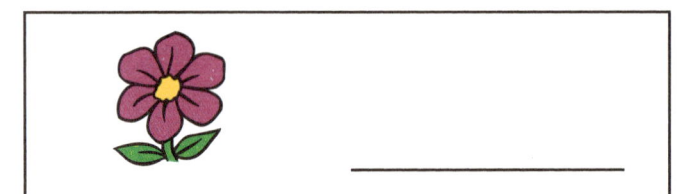

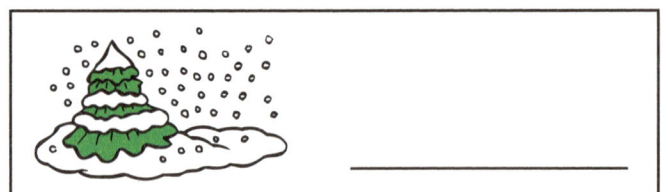

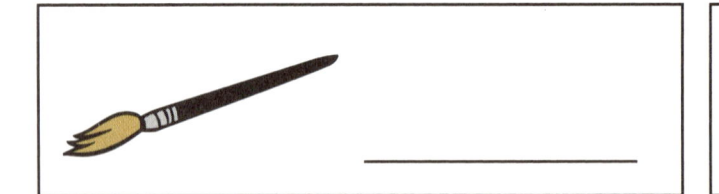

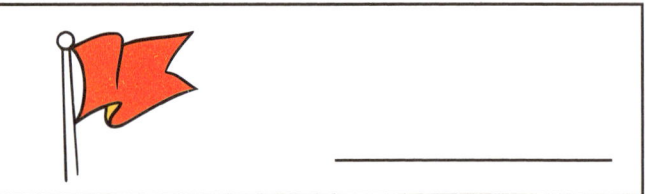

(broom)	_____	(skunk)	_____
(fly)	_____	(branch)	_____
(flower)	_____	(snow)	_____
(brush)	_____	(plate)	_____
(snake)	_____	(flag)	_____
(skate)	_____	(playground)	_____

Reading: Grade 2   10   ©2006 School Specialty Publishing

Name _____

Nothing But Net

Directions: Write the missing consonant blends.

| scr | mp | dr | lp | nk | ss | st | sk | nd | gr | sn | nt | fr | sl |

1. "My ___ ___ eakers he ___ ___ me run very fa ___ ___ !" exclaimed Jim Shooz.

2. "I really like to ___ ___ ibble the ball," announced Dub L. Dribble.

3. Team captain ___ ___ y-High Hook can easily ___ ___ am du ___ ___ the basketball into the net.

4. Will Kenny Dooit make an extra poi ___ ___ with his ___ ___ ee throw?

5. Harry Leggs can ju ___ ___ at lea ___ ___ 4 feet off the ___ ___ ound.

6. Wow! Willie Makeit finally caught the ball on the rebou ___ ___ !

7. "Watch me pa ___ ___ the ball!" yelled Holden Firm.

8. He ju ___ ___ ___ ___ opped the ball, and now they all will ___ ___ ___ amble to get it.

9. "I cannot tell which team will win at the e ___ ___ of the game," decided Ed G. Nerves.

10. "You silly boy! Of course, the team with the mo ___ ___ poi ___ ___ s will win!" explained Kay G. Fann.

©2006 School Specialty Publishing — Reading: Grade 2

Name _____

Consonant Digraph th

Some consonants work together to stand for a new sound. They are called **consonant digraphs**. Listen for the sound of consonant digraph **th** in **think**.

think

Directions: Print **th** under the pictures whose names begin with the sound of **th**. Color the **th** pictures.

Reading: Grade 2   12   ©2006 School Specialty Publishing

Name _____

Read and Write Digraphs

Directions: Write a word from the box to label each picture.

chest	check	sheep
chimp	cherry	thirty
chain	cheese	wheel

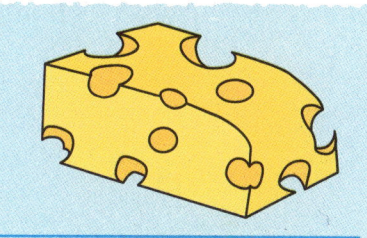

Name _____

Ending Digraphs

Some words end with consonant digraphs. Listen for the ending digraphs in **duck**, **moth**, **dish**, and **branch**.

du**ck**    mo**th**   di**sh** 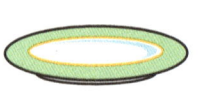   bran**ch**

Directions: Say the name of each picture. Circle the letters that stand for the ending sound.

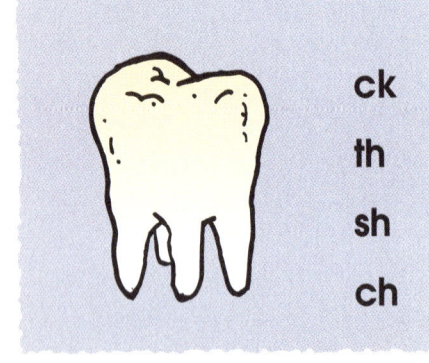

	ck th sh ch		ck th sh wh		ck th sh ch
	ck th sh ch		ck th sh ch	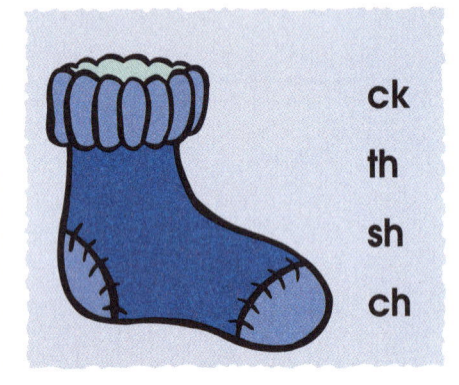	ck th sh ch
	ck th sh ch		ck th sh ch		ck th sh ch

Reading: Grade 2   14   ©2006 School Specialty Publishing

Name_____

Missing Digraphs

Directions: Fill in the circle beside the missing digraph in each word.

___ale
- ○ wh
- ○ wr
- ○ ch

pea___
- ○ ck
- ○ th
- ○ ch

___ife
- ○ kn
- ○ ch
- ○ wr

___imp
- ○ ck
- ○ kn
- ○ ch

___ell
- ○ ch
- ○ sh
- ○ ck

clo___
- ○ ck
- ○ ch
- ○ kn

___ite
- ○ kn
- ○ wr
- ○ th

fi___
- ○ ch
- ○ sh
- ○ th

___orn
- ○ th
- ○ wr
- ○ ch

©2006 School Specialty Publishing · 15 · Reading: Grade 2

Name _____

Silent Letters

Some words have letters you cannot hear at all, such as the **gh** in **night**, the **w** in **wrong**, the **l** in **walk**, the **k** in **knee**, the **b** in **climb**, and the **t** in **listen**.

Directions: Look at the words in the word box. Write the word under its picture. Underline the silent letters.

knife	light	calf	wrench	lamb	eight
wrist	whistle	comb	thumb	knob	knee

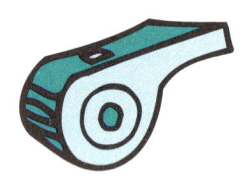

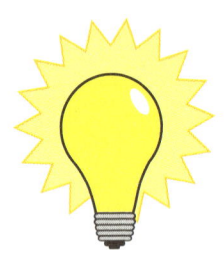

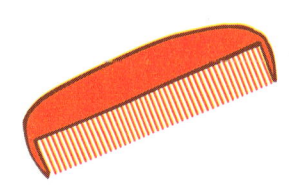

Reading: Grade 2 16 ©2006 School Specialty Publishing

Name _____

Sounds of c and g

Consonants **c** and **g** each have two sounds. Listen for the soft **c** sound in **pencil**. Listen for the hard **c** sound in **cup**.

Listen for the soft **g** sound in **giant**. Listen for the hard **g** sound in **goat**. C and g usually have the soft sound when they are followed by **e**, **i**, or **y**.

Directions: Say the name of each picture. Listen for the sound of **c** or **g**. Then, read the words in each list. Circle the words that have that sound of **c** or **g**.

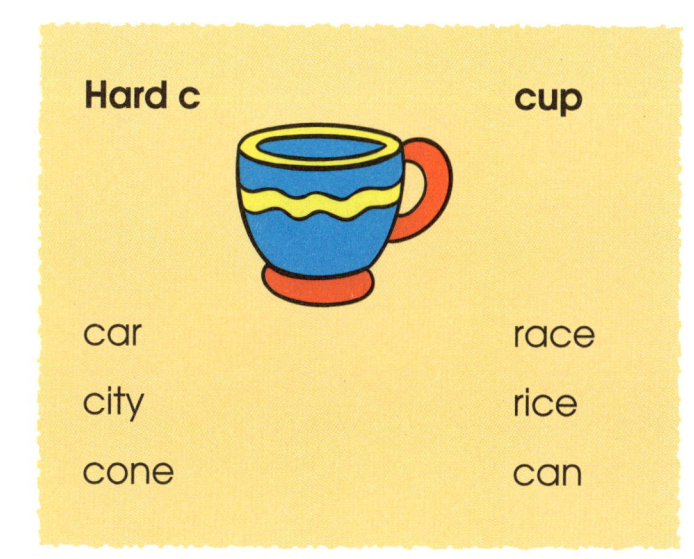

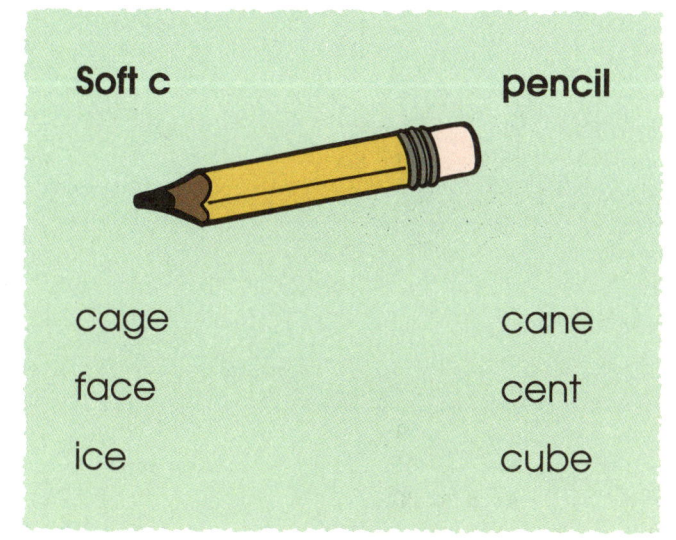

Hard c   cup

car   race
city   rice
cone   can

Soft c   pencil

cage   cane
face   cent
ice   cube

Hard g   goat

good   magic
dragon   gum
stage   gentle

Soft g   giant

garden   gem
page   giraffe
gas   gorilla

Name _____

Hard and Soft c and g

Directions: Underline the letter that follows the **c** or **g** in each word. Write **hard** if the word has the hard **c** or hard **g** sound. Write **soft** if the word has the soft **c** or soft **g** sound.

car	wagon	cup
pencil	gym	cot
giant	gem	celery
gum	cymbals	goat

Reading: Grade 2   18   ©2006 School Specialty Publishing

Name _____

Short Vowel Scrapbook

A Cut-and-Fold Book

Directions: The pages of your Cut-and-Fold Book are on the back of this sheet. First, follow the directions below to make the book. Then, follow the directions on the small pages of your Cut-and-Fold Book. Show your *Short Vowel Scrapbook* to a family member or friend. Think of other words you could draw for each short vowel sound.

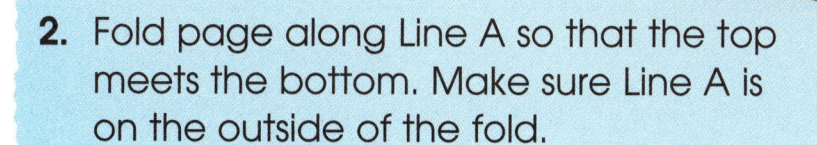

1. Tear the page out of the book.

2. Fold page along Line A so that the top meets the bottom. Make sure Line A is on the outside of the fold.

3. Fold along Line B to make the book.

2

Draw a picture whose name has the short **u** sound.

Draw a picture of something whose name has the short **i** sound.

3

Draw a picture of something whose name has the short **o** sound.

1

Draw a picture of something whose name has the short **a** sound.

4

Draw a picture of something whose name has the short **e** sound.

Name_____

Kick It In!

Directions: Write a vowel to complete each word below.

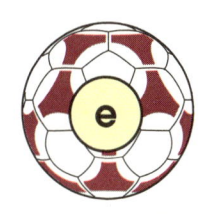

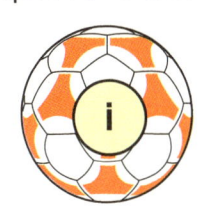

a   e   i   o   u

n__t

p__ss

s__cks

r__n

k__ck

©2006 School Specialty Publishing

21

Reading: Grade 2

Name _____

Long Vowels

Long vowel sounds have the same sound as their names. When a **Super Silent e** comes at the end of a word, you cannot hear it, but it changes the short vowel sound to a long vowel sound.

Examples: rope, skate, bee, pie, cute

Directions: Say the name of the pictures. Listen for the long vowel sounds. Write the missing long vowel sound under each picture.

c ___ ke    h ___ ke 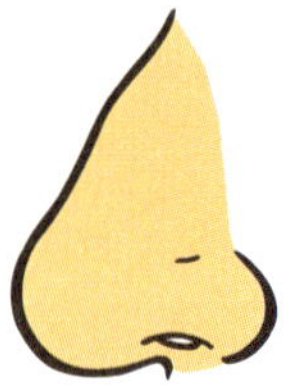   n ___ se

___ pe    c ___ be    gr ___ pe

r ___ ke 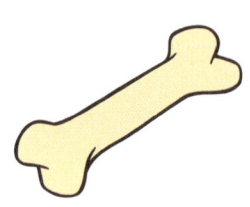   b ___ ne    k ___ te

Reading: Grade 2   22   ©2006 School Specialty Publishing

Name _____

Super Silent e

Long vowel sounds have the same sound as their names. When a **Super Silent e** appears at the end of a word, you cannot hear it, but it makes the other vowel have a long sound. For example: **tub** has a **short** vowel sound, and **tube** has a **long** vowel sound.

Directions: Look at the following pictures. Decide if the word has a short or long vowel sound. Circle the correct word. Watch for the **Super Silent e**!

can   cane    tub   tube    rob   robe    rat   rate

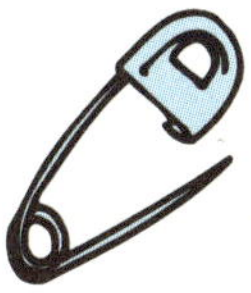

pin   pine    cap   cape    not   note    pan   pane

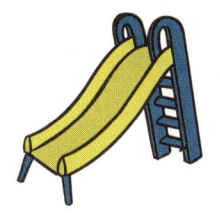

slid   slide    dim   dime    tap   tape    cub   cube

©2006 School Specialty Publishing   23   Reading: Grade 2

Name _____

Review

Directions: Read the words in each box. Cross out the word that does **not** belong.

long vowels	short vowels
cube	man
cup	pet
rake	fix
me	ice

long vowels	short vowels
soap	cat
seed	pin
read	rain
mat	frog

Directions: Write **short** or **long** to label the words in each box.

_____ vowels	_____ vowels
hose	frog
take	hot
bead	sled
cube	lap
eat	block
see	sit

Reading: Grade 2   ©2006 School Specialty Publishing

Name_____

Missing Vowel Pairs

Directions: Fill in the circle beside the missing vowel pair in each word.

t___	tr___	sn___
○ ie ○ ay ○ oa	○ ow ○ ui ○ ay	○ ow ○ ie ○ ay
ch___n	gr___	r___d
○ ie ○ ui ○ ai	○ oa ○ ay ○ ie	○ oa ○ ay ○ ui
b___	fl___s	s___t
○ ai ○ ow ○ ui	○ ai ○ oa ○ ie	○ ui ○ ay ○ ie

©2006 School Specialty Publishing　　　25　　　Reading: Grade 2

Name _____

Missing Vowel Pairs

Directions: Fill in the circle beside the missing vowel pair in each word.

h___	tr___n	s___p
○ ui	○ oa	○ oa
○ ow	○ ai	○ ai
○ ay	○ ie	○ ui

j___ce	p___	cr___
○ ai	○ ui	○ ui
○ ui	○ oa	○ ay
○ ie	○ ie	○ ow

g___t	fr___t	sn___l
○ ai	○ ai	○ ow
○ oa	○ ow	○ ai
○ ui	○ ui	○ ie

Reading: Grade 2   26   ©2006 School Specialty Publishing

Name _____

Y as a Vowel

Y as a vowel can make two sounds. **Y** can make the long sound of **e** or the long sound of **i**.

Directions: Color the spaces:
purple – **y** sounds like **i**.
yellow – **y** sounds like **e**.

What is the picture? _____

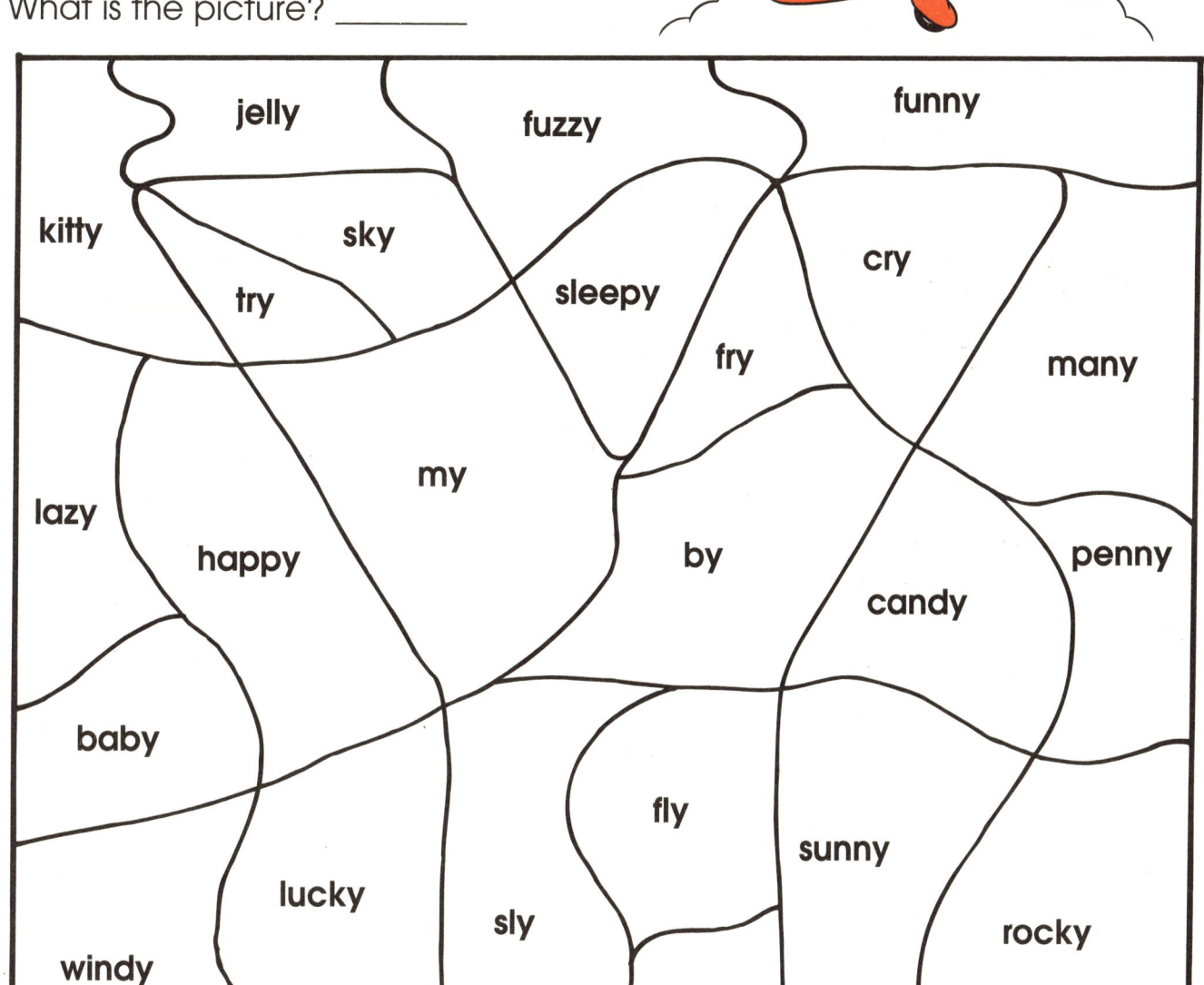

Words in picture
jelly, fuzzy, funny, kitty, sky, cry, try, sleepy, fry, many, my, by, penny, lazy, happy, candy, baby, fly, sunny, lucky, sly, rocky, windy, shy

©2006 School Specialty Publishing

27

Reading: Grade 2

Name _____

Compound Your Effort

A **compound word** is made from two shorter words. An example of a compound word is **sandbox**, made from **sand** and **box**.

Directions: Find one word in the word box that goes with each of the words below to make a compound word. Write the compound words on the lines. Cross out each word that you use.

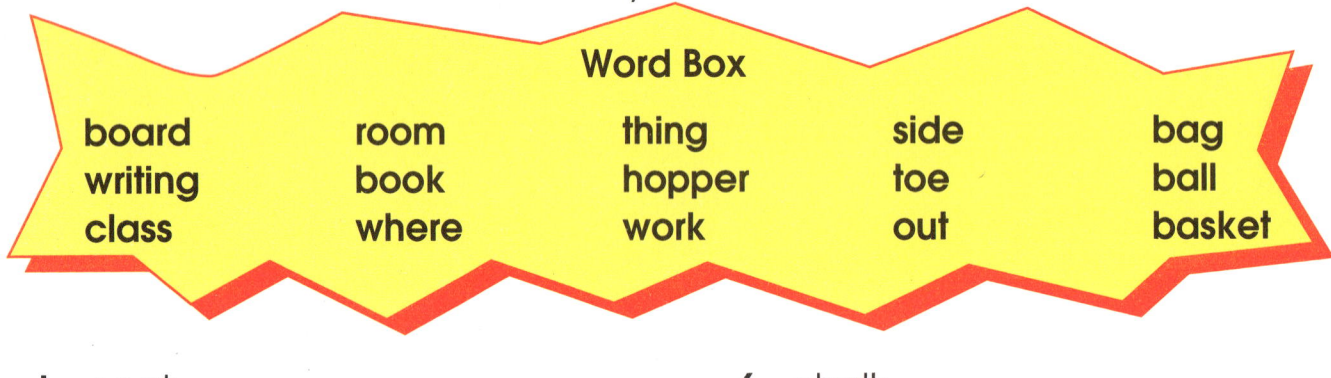

Word Box

board	room	thing	side	bag
writing	book	hopper	toe	ball
class	where	work	out	basket

1. coat _____
2. snow _____
3. home _____
4. waste _____
5. tip _____

6. chalk _____
7. note _____
8. grass _____
9. school _____
10. with _____

Look at the words in the word box that you did **not** use. Use those words to make your own compound words.

1. _____
2. _____
3. _____
4. _____
5. _____

Reading: Grade 2   28   ©2006 School Specialty Publishing

Name _____

Mixing a Compound

sometimes   downtown   girlfriend
everybody   maybe   myself   lunchbox
baseball   outside   today

Directions: Write the correct compound word on the line. Then, use the numbered letters to solve the code.

1. Opposite of inside   __ __ __ __ __ __ __
                                1

2. Another word for *me*   __ __ __ __ __ __
                                 2   3

3. A girl who is a friend __ __ __ __ __ __ __ __ __ __
                            4   5

4. Not yesterday or tomorrow, but . . .   __ __ __ __ __
                                                 6

5. All of the people   __ __ __ __ __ __ __ __ __
                            7   8

6. A sport   __ __ __ __ __ __ __ __
                                   9

7. The main part of a town   __ __ __ __ __ __ __ __
                                     10   11

8. Not always, just . . .   __ __ __ __ __ __ __ __ __
                             12   13

9. A box for carrying your lunch   __ __ __ __ __ __ __ __
                                             14

10. Perhaps or might   __ __ __ __ __
                                   15

__ __ __ __ __ __ __ __ __ ! __ __ __
10 8 11 6 15 7 3 1 9   2 8 1

__ __ __ __ __ __ __ __
3 8 1 11 6 13 14 15

__ __ __ __ __   __ __ __ __ __ __ __ __ !
7 5 4 14 13   12 8 9 1 13 5 8 11

Name _____

Prefix re

A **prefix** is a word part. It is added to the beginning of a base word to change the base word's meaning. The prefix **re** means "again."

Example: **Refill** means "to fill again."

Directions: Look at the pictures. Read the base words. Add the prefix **re** to the base word to show that the action is being done again. Write your new word on the line.

read

write

paint

use

build

pay

Reading: Grade 2

30

©2006 School Specialty Publishing

Prefixes un and dis

The prefixes **un** and **dis** mean "not" or "the opposite of."

Unlocked means "not locked."

Dismount is the opposite of "mount."

Directions: Look at the pictures. Circle the word that tells about the picture. Then, write the word on the line.

tied
untied

like
dislike

happy
unhappy

obey
disobey

safe
unsafe

honest
dishonest

Name _____

Suffixes ful, less, ness, ly

A **suffix** is a word part that is added at the end of a base word to change the base word's meaning. Look at the suffixes below.

The suffix **ful** means "full of." **Cheerful** means "full of cheer."

The suffix **less** means "without." **Cloudless** means "without clouds."

The suffix **ness** means "a state of being." **Darkness** means "being dark."

The suffix **ly** means "in this way." **Slowly** means "in a slow way."

Directions: Add the suffixes to the base words to make new words.

care + ful =

pain + less =

brave + ly =

sad + ly =

sick + ness =

Name _____

Suffixes and Meanings

Remember: The suffix **ful** means "full of."

The suffix **less** means "without."

The suffix **ness** means "a state of being."

The suffix **ly** means "in this way."

The sun shines **brightly**.

Directions: Write the word that matches the meaning.

without pain

in a quick way

in a neat way

without fear

full of grace

the state of being soft

the state of being sick

in a glad way

©2006 School Specialty Publishing

Reading: Grade 2

Name _____

Suffixes er and est

Suffixes **er** and **est** can be used to compare. Use **er** when you compare two things. Use **est** when you compare more than two things.

Example: The puppy is small**er** than its mom.
    This puppy is the small**est** puppy in the litter.

Directions: Add the suffixes to the base words to make words that compare.

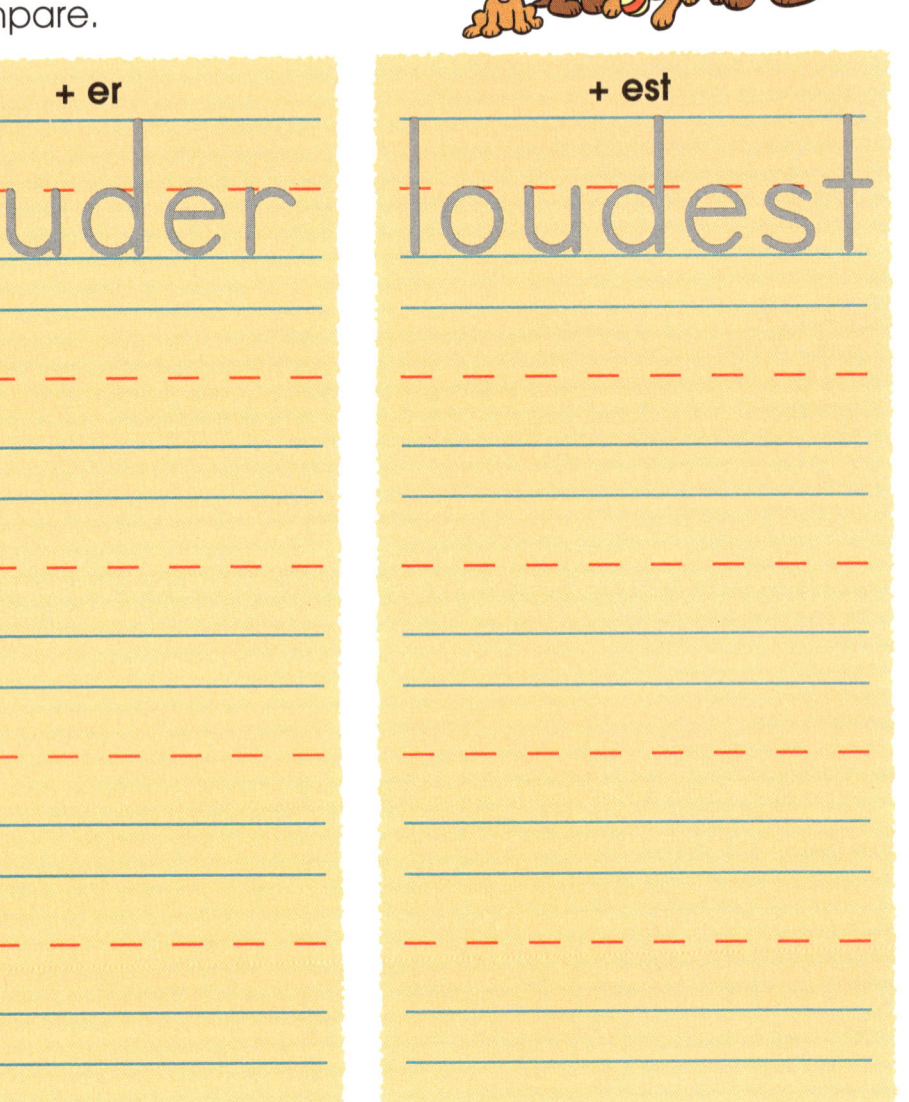

Base Word	+ er	+ est
1. loud	louder	loudest
2. old		
3. neat		
4. fast		
5. kind		
6. tall		

Reading: Grade 2

Name _____

Scale the Synonym Slope

Synonyms are words that have almost the same meaning. **Tired** and **sleepy** are synonyms. **Talk** and **speak** are synonyms.

Directions: Read the word. Find its synonym on the hill. Write the synonym on the line.

1. glad _____

2. little _____

3. begin _____

4. above _____

5. damp _____

6. large _____

wet

big

happy

over

small

start

©2006 School Specialty Publishing

Reading: Grade 2

Name _____

We Go Together!

Directions: Circle the two words in each line that have almost the same meaning.

1. gooey   sticky   hard

2. slow   hurry   rush

3. slope   hill   sled

4. stop   red   end

5. treat   pledge   promise

6. piece   bit   pie

7. excuse   easy   simple

8. complete   whole   pile

Reading: Grade 2   36   ©2006 School Specialty Publishing

Name_____

Amazing Antonyms

Antonyms are words that have opposite meanings. **Old** and **new** are antonyms. **Laugh** and **cry** are antonyms, too.

Directions: Below each word, write its antonym. Use words from the word box.

down
go
left
sad
dry

stop

happy

right

up

wet

©2006 School Specialty Publishing   37   Reading: Grade 2

Name _____

Trading Places

Directions: In each sentence below, circle the incorrect word. Then, rewrite the sentence replacing the circled word with its **antonym** from the word list. The first one has been done for you.

Word List
happy　　tall
full　　　tie
loud　　 lock
dangerous

Swimming in the dark was (safe).
Swimming in the dark was dangerous.

The gorilla's scream sounded very quiet.

_____

The packed room was empty.

_____

My 6-foot brother is very short.

_____

George, the funny clown, makes me very unhappy.

_____

In an unsafe place, you should always unlock the door.

_____

You need to untie your shoes before you run.

_____

Reading: Grade 2　　　　　　　　　　©2006 School Specialty Publishing

Name _____

Antonym or Synonym?

Directions: Use **yellow** to color the spaces that have word pairs that are **antonyms**. Use **blue** to color the spaces that have word pairs that are **synonyms**.

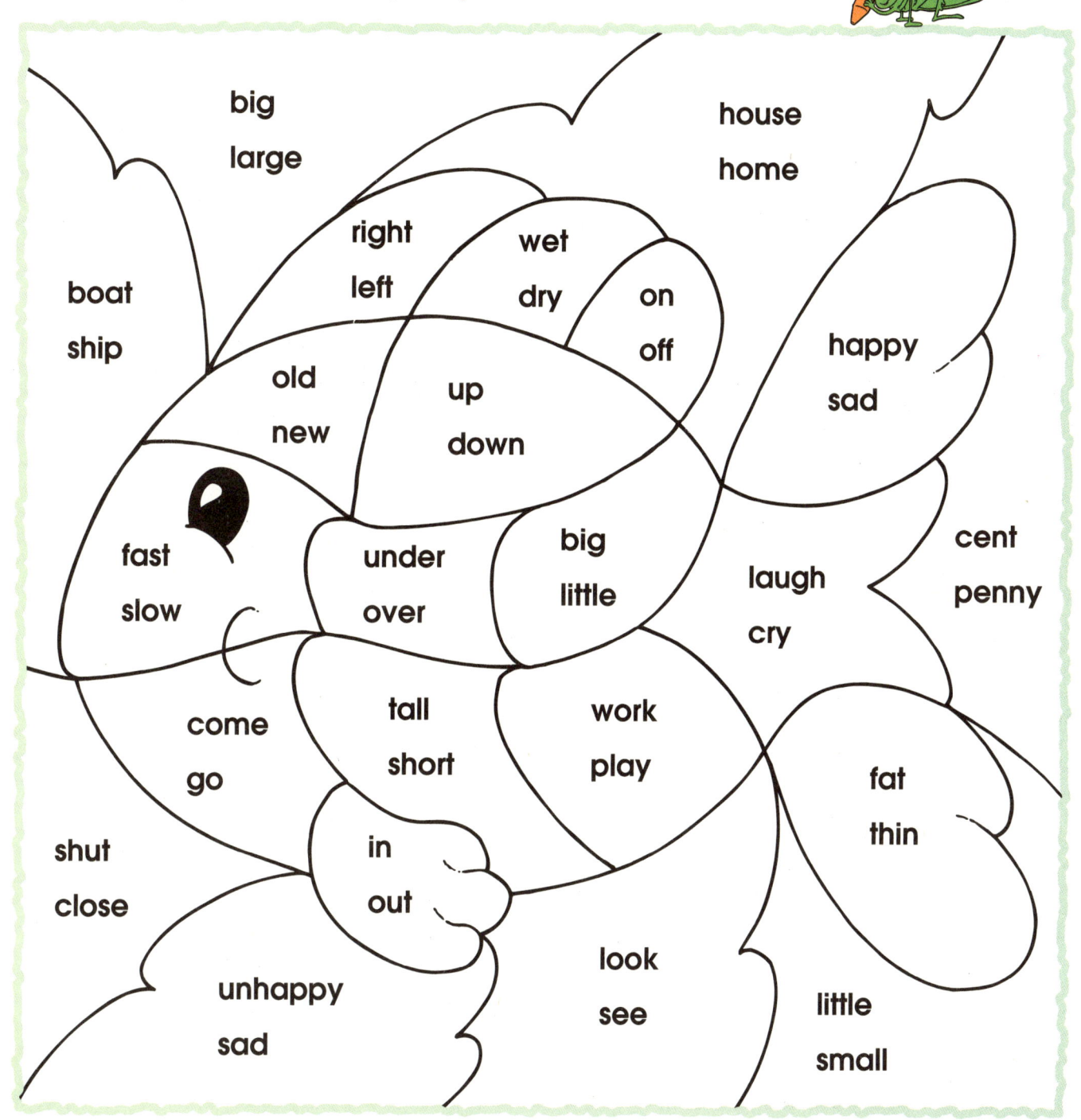

- big / large
- house / home
- right / left
- wet / dry
- on / off
- boat / ship
- old / new
- up / down
- happy / sad
- fast / slow
- under / over
- big / little
- laugh / cry
- cent / penny
- come / go
- tall / short
- work / play
- fat / thin
- shut / close
- in / out
- look / see
- unhappy / sad
- little / small

©2006 School Specialty Publishing

39

Reading: Grade 2

Name _____

Contractions

A **contraction** is a word made up of two words joined together with one or more letters left out. An **apostrophe** is used in place of the missing letters.

Examples: I am—**I'm**
do not—**don't**
that is—**that's**

Directions: Draw a line to match each contraction to the words from which it was made. The first one is done for you.

1. he's — we are
2. we're — cannot
3. can't — he is
4. I'll — she is
5. she's — I will

6. they'll — are not
7. aren't — they will
8. I've — you have
9. you've — will not
10. won't — I have

Directions: Write the contraction for each pair of words.

1. you are _____
2. does not _____
3. do not _____
4. would not _____

5. she is _____
6. we have _____
7. has not _____
8. did not _____

Name _____

Something Is Missing!

doesn't   it's   she's
don't   aren't   who's   he's
didn't   that's   isn't

Directions: Write the correct contraction for each set of words. Then, circle the letter that was left out when the contraction was made.

1. he is _____
2. are not _____
3. do not _____
4. who is _____
5. is not _____

6. did not _____
7. it is _____
8. she is _____
9. does not _____
10. that is _____

Directions: Write the missing contraction on the line.

1. _____ on her way to school.
2. There _____ enough time to finish the story.
3. Do you think _____ too long?
4. We _____ going to the party.
5. Donna _____ like the movie.
6. _____ going to try for a part in the play?
7. Bob said _____ going to run in the big race.
8. They _____ know how to bake a cake.
9. Tom _____ want to go skating on Saturday.
10. Look, _____ where they found the lost watch.

©2006 School Specialty Publishing   41   Reading: Grade 2

Name _____

Common Nouns

A **common noun** names a person, place, or thing.

Example: The **boy** had several **chores** to do.

Directions: Fill in the circle below each common noun.

1. First, the boy had to feed his puppy.
2. He got fresh water for his pet.
3. Next, the boy poured some dry food into a bowl.
4. He set the dish on the floor in the kitchen.
5. Then, he called his dog to come to dinner.
6. The boy and his dad worked in the garden.
7. The father turned the dirt with a shovel.
8. The boy carefully dropped seeds into little holes.
9. Soon, tiny plants would sprout from the soil.
10. Sunshine and showers would help the radishes grow.

Reading: Grade 2

42

©2006 School Specialty Publishing

Name _____

Proper Nouns

A **proper noun** names a specific or certain person, place, or thing. A proper noun always begins with a capital letter.

Example: Becky flew to **St. Louis** in a **Boeing 747**.

Directions: Put a ✔ in front of each proper noun.

_____ 1. uncle

_____ 2. Aunt Retta

_____ 3. Forest Park

_____ 4. Gateway Arch

_____ 5. Missouri

_____ 6. school

_____ 7. Miss Hunter

_____ 8. Northwest Plaza

_____ 9. New York Science Center

_____ 10. Ms. Small

_____ 11. Doctor Chang

_____ 12. Union Station

_____ 13. Henry Shaw

_____ 14. museum

_____ 15. librarian

_____ 16. shopping mall

Directions: Underline the proper nouns.

1. Becky went to visit Uncle Harry.
2. He took her to see the Cardinals play baseball.
3. The game was at Busch Stadium.
4. The St. Louis Cardinals played the Chicago Cubs.
5. Mark McGwire hit a home run.

©2006 School Specialty Publishing

Reading: Grade 2

Name _____

Singular Nouns

A **singular noun** names one person, place, or thing.

Example: My **mother** unlocked the old **trunk** in the **attic**.

Directions: If the noun is singular, draw a line from it to the trunk. If the noun is **not** singular, draw an **X** on the word.

teddy bear	hammer	picture	sweater
bonnet	letters	seashells	fiddle
kite	ring	feather	books
postcard	crayon	doll	dishes
blocks	hats	bicycle	blanket

Reading: Grade 2

©2006 School Specialty Publishing

Name _____

Plural Nouns

A **plural noun** names more than one person, place, or thing.

Example: Some **dinosaurs** ate **plants** in **swamps**.

Directions: Underline each plural noun.

1. Large animals lived millions of years ago.
2. Dinosaurs roamed many parts of the Earth.
3. Scientists look for fossils.
4. The bones can tell a scientist many things.
5. These bones help tell what the creatures were like.
6. Some had curved claws and whip-like tails.
7. Others had beaks and plates of armor.
8. Some dinosaurs lived on the plains, and others lived in forests.
9. You can see the skeletons of dinosaurs at some museums.
10. We often read about these animals in books.

Name _____

Action Verbs

A **verb** is a word that can show action.

Example: I **jump**.   He **kicks**.   He **walked**.

Directions: Underline the verb in each sentence. Write it on the line.

1. Our school plays games on Field Day. _____

2. Juan runs 50 yards. _____

3. Carmen hops in a sack race. _____

4. Paula tosses a ball through a hoop. _____

5. One girl carries a jellybean on a spoon. _____

6. Lola bounces the ball. _____

7. Some boys chase after balloons. _____

8. Mark chooses me for his team. _____

9. The children cheer for the winners. _____

10. Everyone enjoys Field Day. _____

Reading: Grade 2 ©2006 School Specialty Publishing

Name _____

Better Sentences

Directions: Describing words like adjectives can make a better sentence. Write a word on each line to make the sentences more interesting. Draw pictures of your sentences.

1. The skater won a medal.

   The _____ skater won a _____ medal.

2. The jewels were in the safe.

   The _____ jewels were in the _____ safe.

3. The airplane flew through the storm.

   The _____ airplane flew through the _____ storm.

4. A fireman rushed into the house.

   A _____ fireman rushed into the _____ house.

5. The detective hid behind the tree.

   The _____ detective hid behind the _____ tree.

©2006 School Specialty Publishing

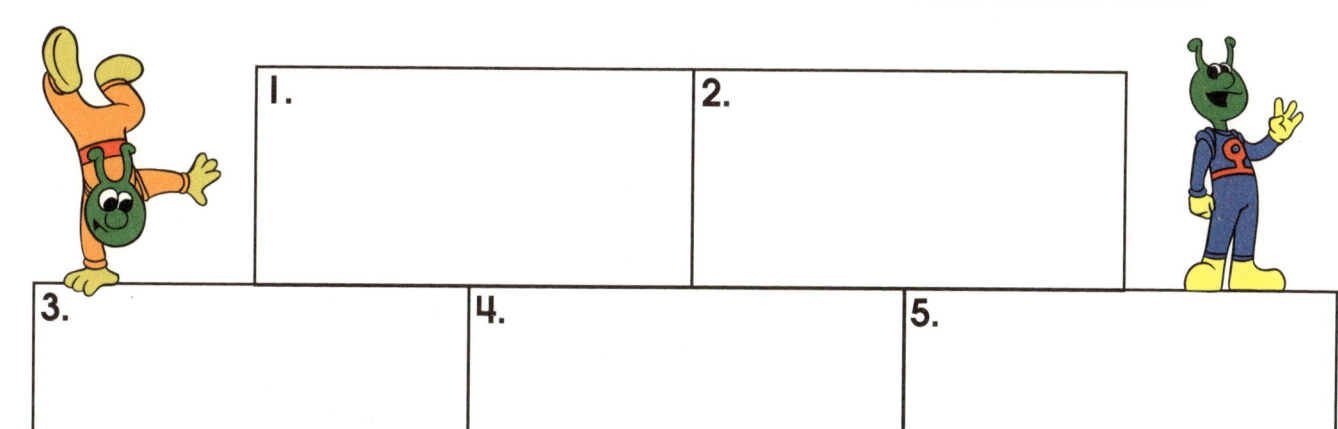

Reading: Grade 2

Name _____

Kinds of Sentences

A **statement** ends with a period. **.**   A **question** ends with a question mark. **?**

Directions: Write the correct mark in each box.

1. Would you like to help me make an aquarium ☐

2. We can use my brother's big fish tank ☐

3. Will you put this colored sand in the bottom ☐

4. I have three shells to put on the sand ☐

5. Can we use your little toy boat, too ☐

6. Let's go buy some fish for our aquarium ☐

7. Will twelve fish be enough ☐

8. Look, they seem to like their new home ☐

9. How often do we give them fish food ☐

10. Let's tell our friends about our new aquarium ☐

Reading: Grade 2   48   ©2006 School Specialty Publishing

Name _____

Four Kinds of Sentences

A **statement** tells something. A **question** asks something. An **exclamation** shows surprise or strong feeling. A **command** tells someone to do something.

Example: The shuttle is ready for takeoff. (statement)
Are all systems go? (question)
What a sight! (exclamation)
Take a picture of this. (command)

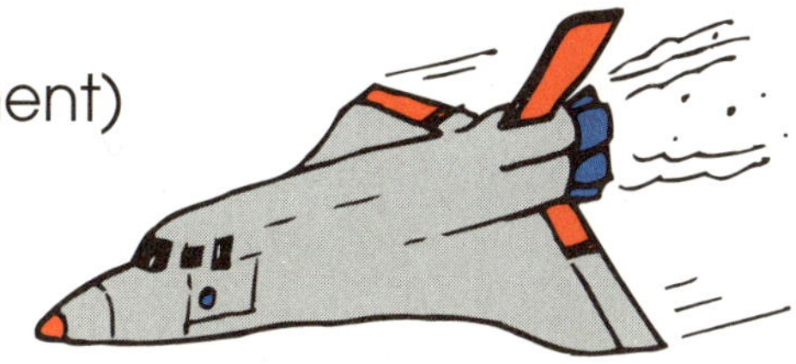

Directions: Use the code to color the spaces.

Code
statement—**yellow**
question—**red**
exclamation—**blue**
command—**gray**

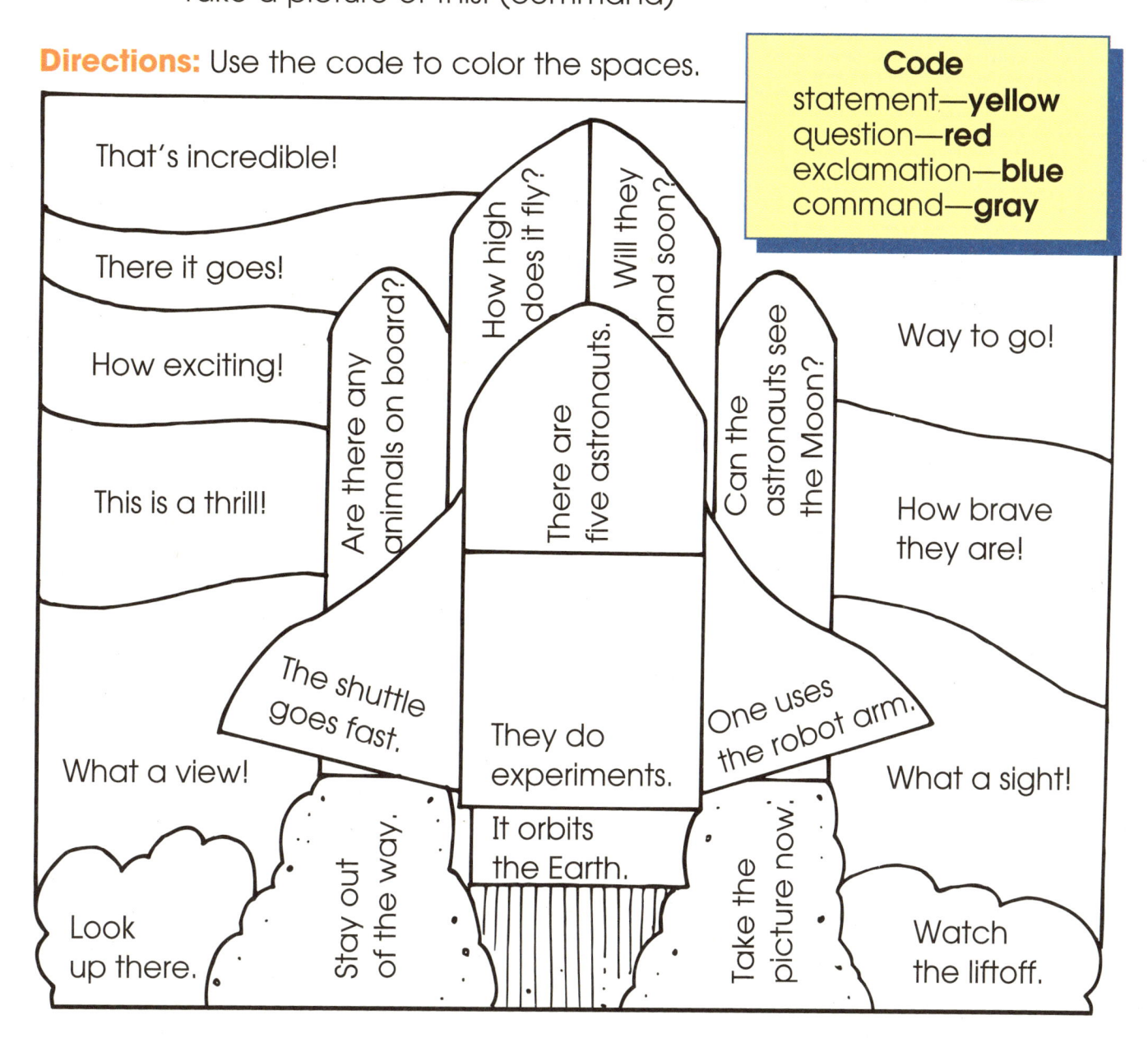

That's incredible!
There it goes!
How exciting!
This is a thrill!
What a view!
Look up there.
Are there any animals on board?
How high does it fly?
Will they land soon?
There are five astronauts.
Can the astronauts see the Moon?
The shuttle goes fast.
They do experiments.
One uses the robot arm.
It orbits the Earth.
Stay out of the way.
Take the picture now.
Way to go!
How brave they are!
What a sight!
Watch the liftoff.

©2006 School Specialty Publishing   49   Reading: Grade 2

Name _____

My Bag's Ready!

The first letter of a word is used to put words in alphabetical (ABC) order.

Directions: Write the golf words below in ABC order. If two or more words begin with the same letter, go to the next letter to put them in ABC order.

club   tee   bag   ball   scorecard   cart   towel

1. _____
2. _____
3. _____
4. _____
5. _____
6. _____
7. _____

Reading: Grade 2   ©2006 School Specialty Publishing

Name _____

Slam Dunk!

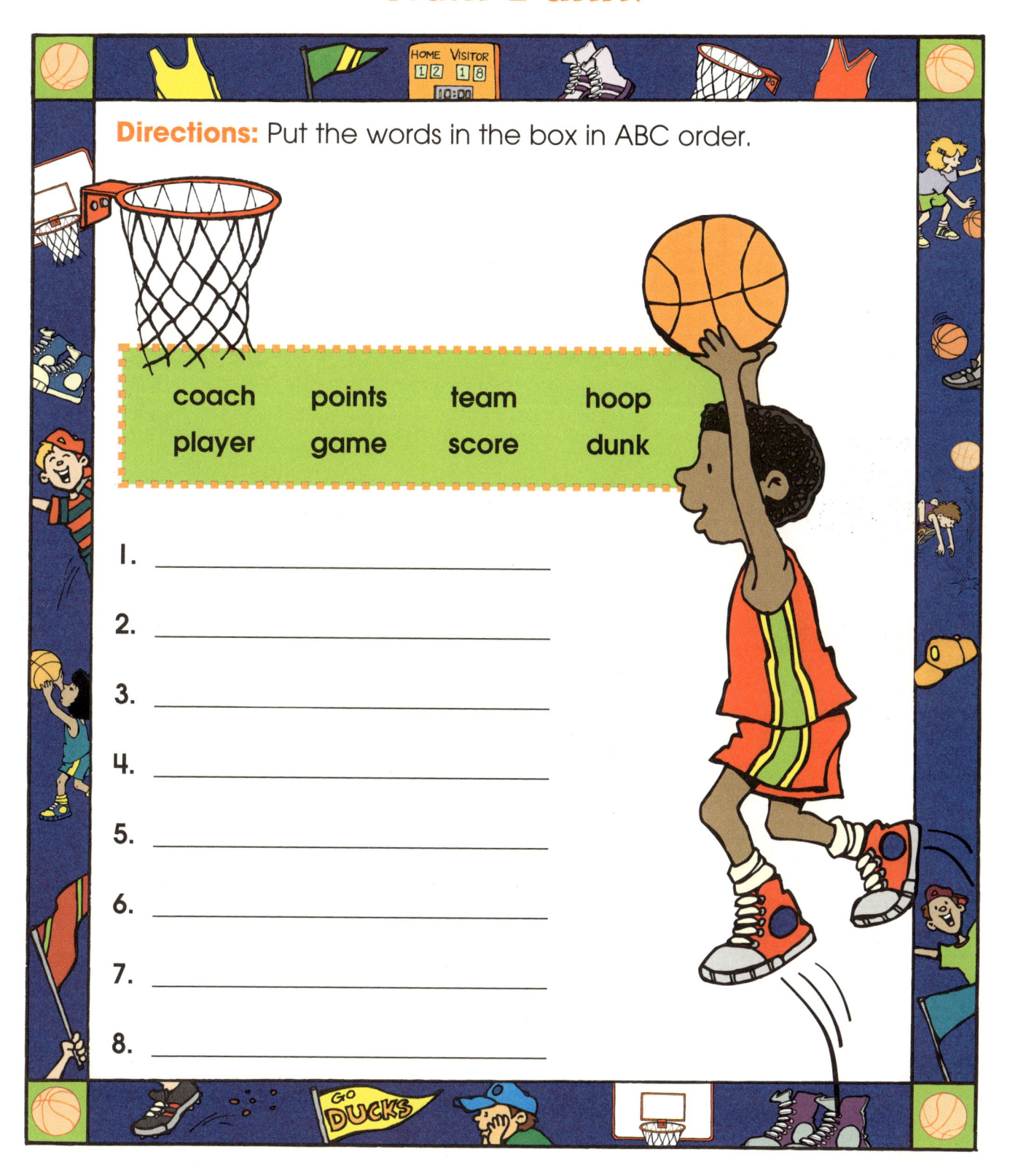

Directions: Put the words in the box in ABC order.

| coach | points | team | hoop |
| player | game | score | dunk |

1. _____
2. _____
3. _____
4. _____
5. _____
6. _____
7. _____
8. _____

©2006 School Specialty Publishing   51   Reading: Grade 2

Name _____

Clue Caper!

Directions: Read the clues below. Write each child's name under the correct picture. Color the hats using the following clues.

_____   _____   _____   _____

- Anna is tall and wearing a green top hat. There is a red baseball cap on top of her top hat!

- Sara is short and wearing a blue polka dotted hat.

- Talia has long hair and is standing between Anna and Sara. Talia is wearing a pretty ribbon in her hair with a flower on it.

- Kessia is standing next to Sara. She is wearing a white baker's hat with a purple veil!

How many hats do you count on the page? _____

Reading: Grade 2   52   ©2006 School Specialty Publishing

Name _____

Make the Touchdown!

Directions: Read the directions. Draw a line as you move from space to space.

1. Start at the football player running with the football.
2. Go up 2 spaces.
3. Go right 3 spaces. Oops!
4. Now, go down 3 spaces.
5. Hurry and go left 1 space.
6. Turn and go down 2 spaces.
7. Now, quickly turn right and go 3 spaces.
8. You were almost tackled. Go up 3 spaces.
9. Move quickly to the right 1 space.
10. Hurray! You made the touchdown!

Directions: Draw a brown football under the goalpost.

©2006 School Specialty Publishing   Reading: Grade 2

Name _____

Game Story

Directions: Put the basketball story in order. Write the numbers **1–5** on the blanks to show when each event happened.

_____ At the end of the regulation game, the score was tied.

_____ The teams warmed up before the game.

_____ The score at the half was Cougars, 25; Lions, 20.

_____ Kim made the first basket of the game.

_____ When the overtime ended, the Lions had won the game 50–49.

Name _____

Story Sequence

Look at picture number 4. What do you think happened before Danny went to the amusement park? What might happen when he is at the amusement park?

Directions: You get to decide how the story will go from beginning to end. Write a number in the empty square in each of the other pictures. Choose any number from 1 through 7 (except 4). Number 1 will be what happened first. Number 7 will be what you think happened last.

©2006 School Specialty Publishing   55   Reading: Grade 2

Name _____

Same/Different: Venn Diagram

A **Venn diagram** is a diagram that shows how two things are the same and different.

Directions: Choose two outdoor sports. Then, follow the instructions to complete the Venn diagram.

1. Write the first sport name under the first circle. Write some words that describe the sport. Write them in the first circle.

2. Write the second sport name under the second circle. Write some words that describe the sport. Write them in the second circle.

3. Where the 2 circles overlap, write some words that describe both sports.

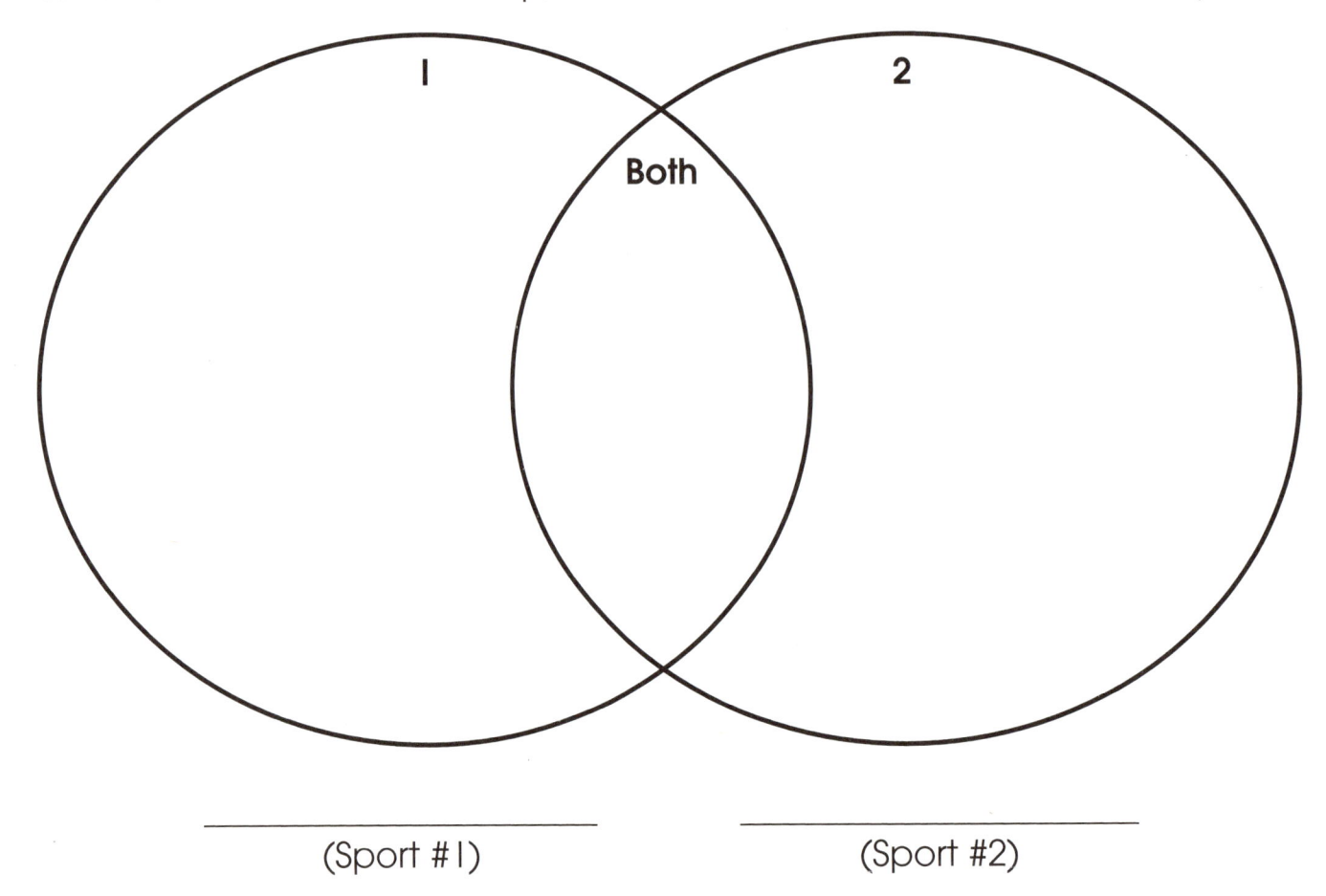

_____   _____
(Sport #1)   (Sport #2)

Reading: Grade 2

Name _____

Same/Different: Ann and Lee Have Fun

Directions: Read about Ann and Lee. Then, write how they are the same and different in the Venn diagram.

Ann and Lee like to play ball. They like to jump rope. Lee likes to play a card game called "Old Maid." Ann likes to play a card game called "Go Fish."

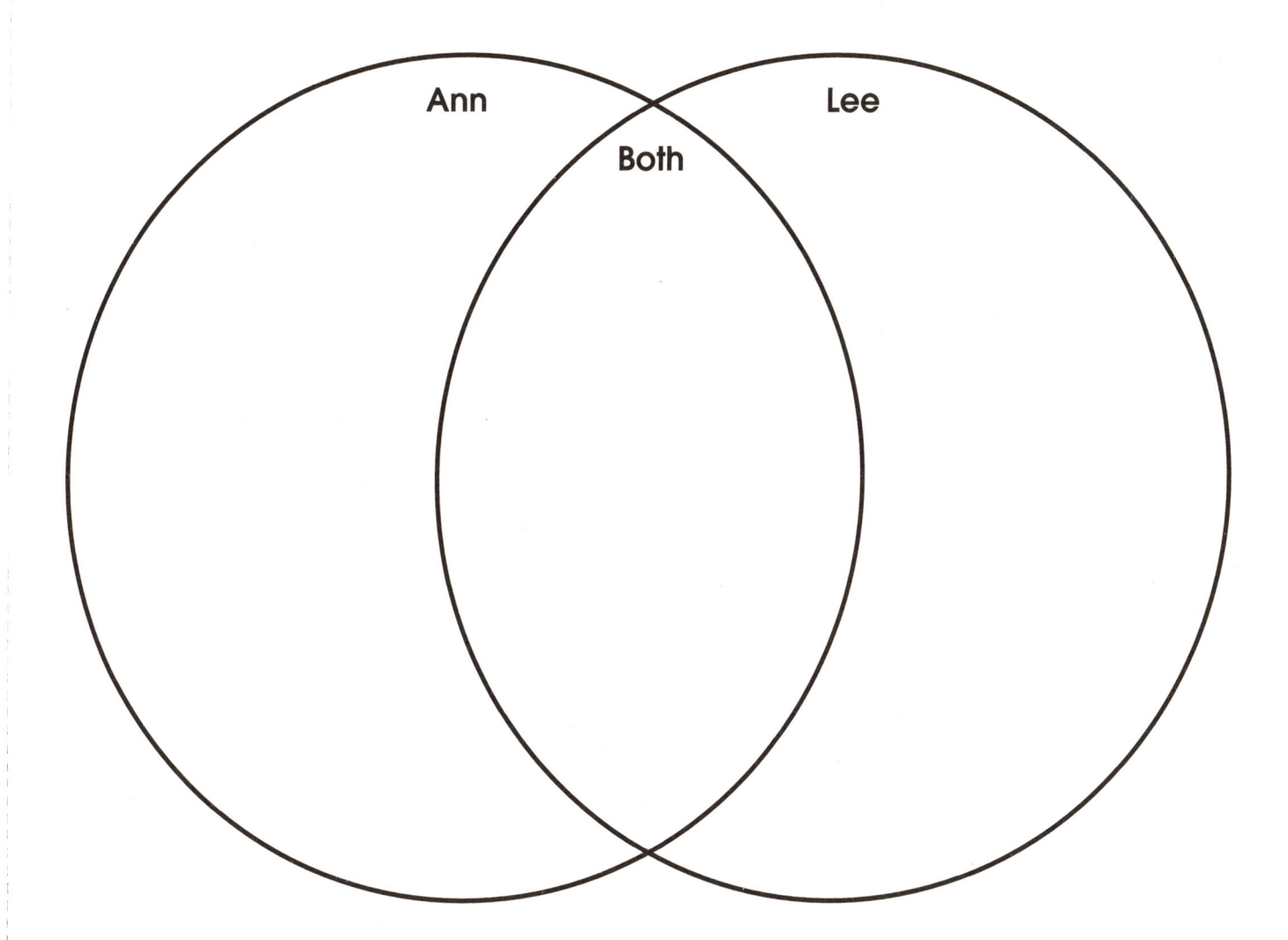

Ann   Lee

Both

©2006 School Specialty Publishing   57   Reading: Grade 2

Name _____

Classifying

Sometimes, you want to put things in groups. One way to put things in groups is to sort them by how they are alike. When you put things together that are alike in some way, you classify them.

You can classify the things in your room. In one group, you can put toys and fun things. In the other group, you can put things that you wear.

Directions: Look at the words on the bedroom door. Put the toys and playthings in the toy box. Put the things you wear in the dresser drawers.

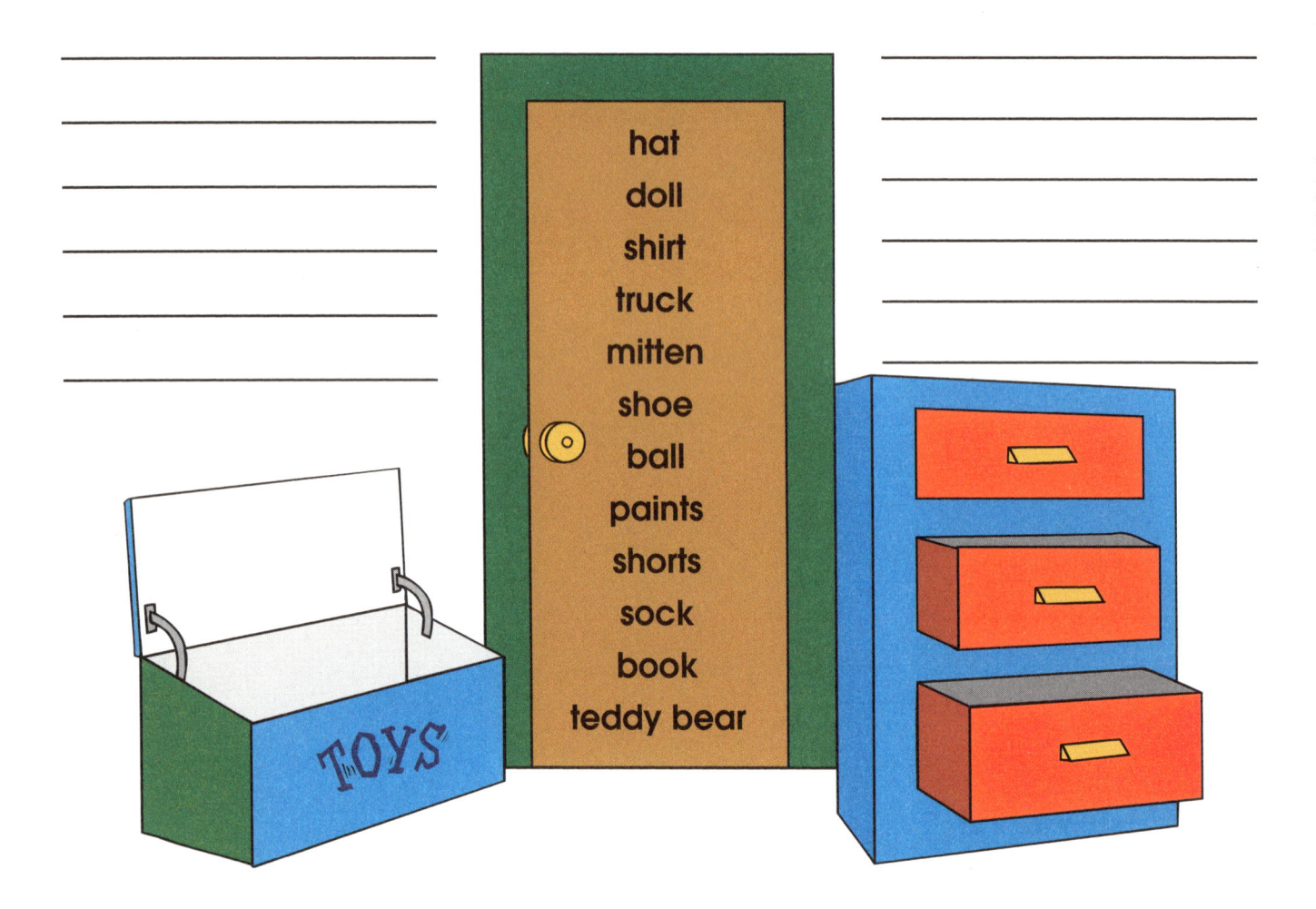

hat
doll
shirt
truck
mitten
shoe
ball
paints
shorts
sock
book
teddy bear

Reading: Grade 2

Name _____

Birds

There are many kinds of birds. The cardinal is a red bird. The cardinal lays three or four eggs. The brown-headed cowbird is black with a brown head. The hummingbird is a very small bird. It lays two eggs. The bald eagle is a large bird. It is brown with a white head. The bald eagle lays from one to four eggs. Bluebirds are blue with orange or light blue breasts. The bluebird lays up to six eggs.

Directions: In the story above, the underlined words are called **adjectives**. Put these describing words in the nests where they belong.

Color

Size

Number

©2006 School Specialty Publishing

59

Reading: Grade 2

Name _____

Cathy Uses Context Clues

When you read, it is important to know about context clues. **Context clues** can help you figure out the meaning of a word, or a missing word, just by looking at the **other words** in the sentence.

Directions: Read each sentence below. Circle the context clues, or other words in the sentence that give you hints.

Write the answer that fits in each blank. The first one is done for you.

1. The (joke) was so ____funny____ I couldn't stop (laughing.)

   bad   long   nice   funny

   The correct answer is **funny** because of the context clues **joke** and **laughing**. They are hints that go best with the word **funny**. Now you try it.

2. We baked a sweet cinnamon apple pie. It smelled _____.

   sour   delicious   funny   odd

3. You have such a long walk home. Do you need a _____ home from school?

   letter   balloon   ride   scooter

4. My brother loves to _____. He has visited over fifty different countries!

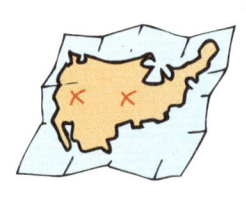

   travel   shout   buy   play

Reading: Grade 2   ©2006 School Specialty Publishing

Name_____

Cathy Uses More Context Clues

When you read, it is important to know about context clues. **Context clues** can help you figure out the meaning of a word, or a missing word, just by looking at the **other words** in the sentence.

Directions: Read each sentence below. Circle the context clues.

Write the answer that fits in each blank.

1. I am a very good _____. I love to draw, paint, and sculpt. My art teacher says I have a lot of talent.

    teacher   boss   captain   artist

2. Playing the _____ is fun. I like to sit on the bench and press those black and white keys.

    violin   piano   rubberband   desk

3. The telephone rings so _____ in my house that I can never fall asleep.

    softly   beautifully   loudly   ugly

4. Summer is my _____ season because I go to camp and have fun!

    favorite   hungry   bad   study

5. The eagle flew so _____ that it looked like a dot in the sky.

    middle   low   high   deep

©2006 School Specialty Publishing   61   Reading: Grade 2

Name _____

Comprehension: Ladybugs

Directions: Read about ladybugs. Then, answer the questions.

  Have you ever seen a ladybug? Ladybugs are red. They have black spots. They have six legs. Ladybugs are pretty!

1. What color are ladybugs? _____

2. What color are their spots? _____

3. How many legs do ladybugs have? _____

Reading: Grade 2

Name_____

The Statue of Liberty

The Statue of Liberty is a symbol of the United States. It stands for freedom. It is the tallest statue in the United States.

The statue is of a woman wearing a robe. She is holding a torch in her right hand. She is holding a book in her left hand. She is wearing a crown. The Statue of Liberty was a gift from the country of France.

Each year, people come from all over the world to visit the statue. Not only do they look at it, they can also go inside the statue. At one time, visitors could go all the way up into the arm. In 1916, the arm was closed to visitors because it was too dangerous. The Statue of Liberty is located on an island in New York Harbor.

Directions: Read the facts above. Then, read each sentence below. If it is true, put a **T** on the line. If it is false, put an **F** on the line.

_____ 1. The Statue of Liberty is a symbol of the United States.

_____ 2. People cannot go inside the statue.

_____ 3. The statue was a gift from Mexico.

_____ 4. People used to be able to climb up into the statue's arm.

_____ 5. It is a very short statue.

_____ 6. The woman statue has a torch in her right hand.

_____ 7. People come from all over to see the statue.

©2006 School Specialty Publishing

Reading: Grade 2

Name _____

Main Idea

The **main idea** tells about the **whole story**.

Directions: Read the story carefully. Then, write a sentence that tells the main idea.

My brother, Scott, loves to fly planes. He flies planes every chance he gets. His favorite type of plane is a Cessna 182. He also likes to go scuba diving. He likes to go scuba diving in the Gulf of Mexico best. Sometimes, he goes flying in the morning and scuba diving in the afternoon. Scott is very adventurous!

_____

_____

_____

My dad is a very talented musician. He taught himself how to play the piano and now he is an excellent piano player. When people hear him play, they can't believe he has never taken any lessons! People say he has "natural talent," and it's true!

_____

_____

_____

Reading: Grade 2   64   ©2006 School Specialty Publishing

Name_____

What Doesn't Belong?

Directions: Read the sentences under each title. Cross out the sentence that does **not** tell about the main idea.

Fun at the Playground

He runs to the slide.
She plays on the swings.
I clean my room.
They climb the monkey bars.
We sit on the seesaw.

Doing My Homework

I open my book.
I take a bath.
I read the book.
I write the words.
I add the numbers.

Going to the Zoo

The monkeys climb the trees.
The seals eat fish.
The snakes move slowly.
The kitten plays with yarn.
The zebra runs fast.

Eating Dinner

Mother cuts the meat.
Father chews the corn.
Sister drinks the milk.
Brother eats his peas.
Grandmother has a big house.

©2006 School Specialty Publishing
Reading: Grade 2

Name _____

What Will They Do?

Directions: Read each sentence. Fill in the circle beside the best prediction. Then, circle the picture that matches your answer.

The boy is putting on his skates.
○ He will go swimming.
○ He will go skating.

The girl fills her glass with milk.
○ She will drink the milk.
○ She will drink water.

The woman wrote a letter to her friend.
○ She will call her friend on the phone.
○ She will put the letter in the mailbox.

The kids gave Sally a birthday gift.
○ She will open the gift.
○ She will throw the gift away.

Reading: Grade 2

66

©2006 School Specialty Publishing

Name _____

How Will It End?

Directions: Read each story. Fill in the circle beside the sentence that tells what will happen next.

It is a snowy winter night. The lights flicker once, twice, and then they go out. It is cold and dark. Dad finds the flashlight and matches. He brings logs in from outside. What will Dad do?

◯ Dad will make a fire.
◯ Dad will cook dinner.
◯ Dad will clean the fireplace.

Maggie has a garden. She likes fresh, homegrown vegetables. She says they make salads taste better. Maggie is going to make a salad for a picnic. What will Maggie do?

◯ Maggie will buy the salad at the store.
◯ Maggie will buy the vegetables at the store.
◯ Maggie will use vegetables from her garden.

The big white goose wakes up. It stands and stretches its wings. It looks all around. It feels very hungry. What will the goose do?

◯ The goose will go swimming.
◯ The goose will look for food.
◯ The goose will go back to sleep.

Name _____

Clues to Conclusions

Directions: Read each story. Fill in the circle beside the correct conclusion.

Joe tried to read the book. He pulled it closer to his face and squinted. What is wrong?

○ The book isn't very interesting.
○ Joe needs glasses.
○ The book is closed.

"My shoes are too tight," said Eddie, "and my pants are too short!" What has happened?

○ Eddie has put on his older brother's clothes.
○ Eddie has become shorter.
○ Eddie has grown.

Patsy went to the beach. She stayed outside for hours. When she came home, she looked in the mirror. Her face was very red. Why did she look different?

○ Patsy had gotten a bad sunburn.
○ Patsy got red paint all over herself.
○ Patsy was very cold.

Reading: Grade 2

©2006 School Specialty Publishing

Name _____

Extra! Extra! Read All About It!

Newspaper reporters have very important jobs. They have to catch a reader's attention and, at the same time, **tell the facts**.

Newspaper reporters write their stories by answering **who**, **what**, **where**, **when**, **why**, and **how**.

Directions: Think about a book you just read and answer the questions below.

Who: **Who** is the story about?

_____

What: **What** happened to the main character?

_____

Where: **Where** does the story take place?

_____

When: **When** does the story take place?

_____

Why: **Why** do these story events happen?

_____

How: **How** do these events happen?

_____

©2006 School Specialty Publishing — Reading: Grade 2

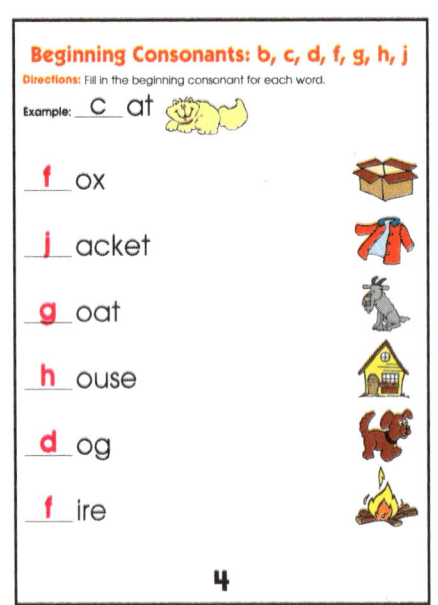

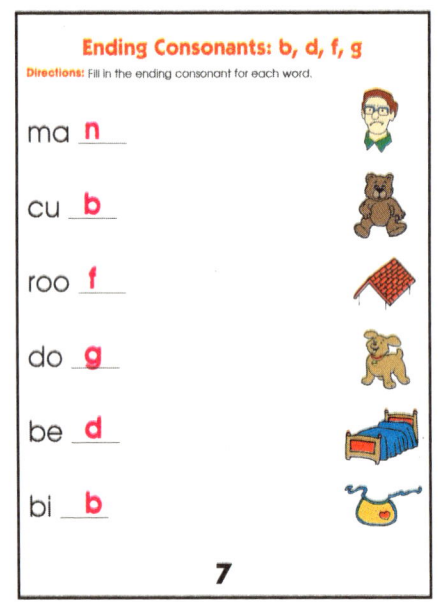

Batter Up!

What did Bobby yell to the batter?

Directions: To find out, say the name of each picture. On the line, write the letter that you hear at the beginning of each picture.

h i t a
h o m e r u n!

Beginning Consonants: b, c, d, f, g, h, j

Directions: Fill in the beginning consonant for each word.

Example: **c** at

f ox
j acket
g oat
h ouse
d og
f ire

Beginning Consonants: k, l, m, n, p, q, r

Directions: Write the letter that makes the beginning sound for each picture.

k   q   r   n
m   l   k   r
q   p   n   m
l   k   r   p

Beginning Consonants: s, t, v, w, x, y, z

Directions: Write the letter under each picture that makes the beginning sound.

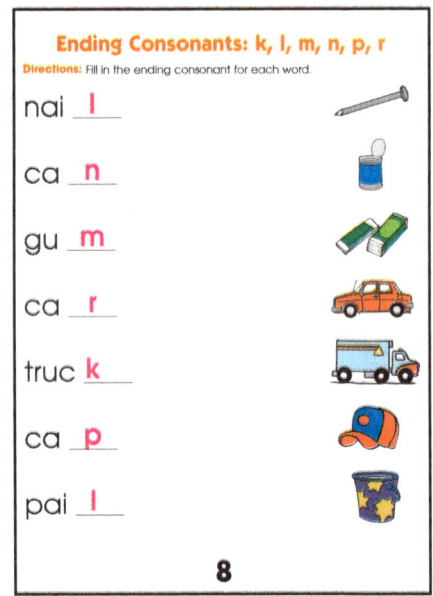

s   z   x
v   y
w   t

Ending Consonants: b, d, f, g

Directions: Fill in the ending consonant for each word.

ma **n**
cu **b**
roo **f**
do **g**
be **d**
bi **b**

Ending Consonants: k, l, m, n, p, r

Directions: Fill in the ending consonant for each word.

nai **l**
ca **n**
gu **m**
ca **r**
truc **k**
ca **p**
pai **l**

Reading: Grade 2 70 ©2006 School Specialty Publishing

Ending Consonants: s, t, x

Directions: Fill in the ending consonant for each word.

ca __t__

bo __x__

bu __s__

fo __x__

boa __t__

ma __t__

9

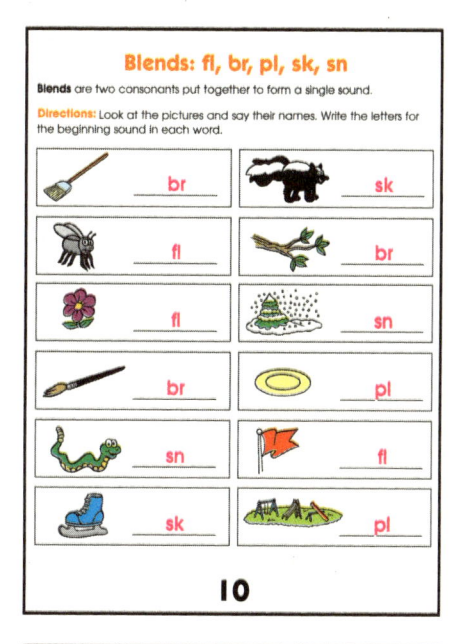

Blends: fl, br, pl, sk, sn

Blends are two consonants put together to form a single sound.

Directions: Look at the pictures and say their names. Write the letters for the beginning sound in each word.

__br__	__sk__
__fl__	__br__
__fl__	__sn__
__br__	__pl__
__sn__	__fl__
__sk__	__pl__

10

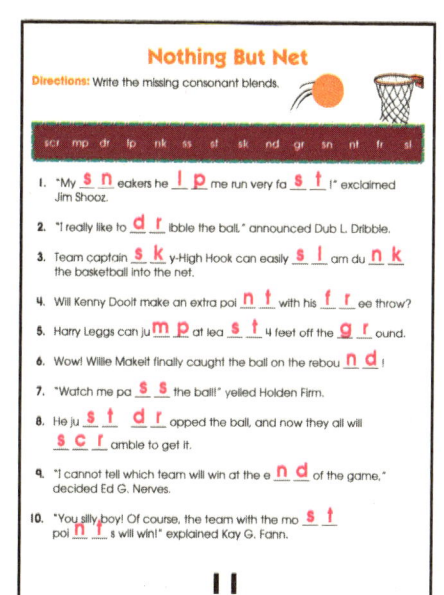

Nothing But Net

Directions: Write the missing consonant blends.

scr mp dr tp nk ss st sk nd gr sn nt fr sl

1. "My __sn__ eakers he __lp__ me run very fa __st__!" exclaimed Jim Shooz.
2. "I really like to __dr__ ibble the ball." announced Dub L. Dribble.
3. Team captain __sk__ y-High Hook can easily __sl__ am du __nk__ the basketball into the net.
4. Will Kenny Dooit make an extra poi __nt__ with his __fr__ ee throw?
5. Harry Leggs can ju __mp__ at lea __st__ 4 feet off the __gr__ ound.
6. Wow! Willie Makeit finally caught the ball on the rebou __nd__!
7. "Watch me pa __ss__ the ball," yelled Holden Firm.
8. He ju __st__ __dr__ opped the ball, and now they all will __scr__ amble to get it.
9. "I cannot tell which team will win at the e __nd__ of the game," decided Ed G. Nerves.
10. "You silly boy! Of course, the team with the mo __st__ poi __nt__ s will win!" explained Kay G. Fann.

11

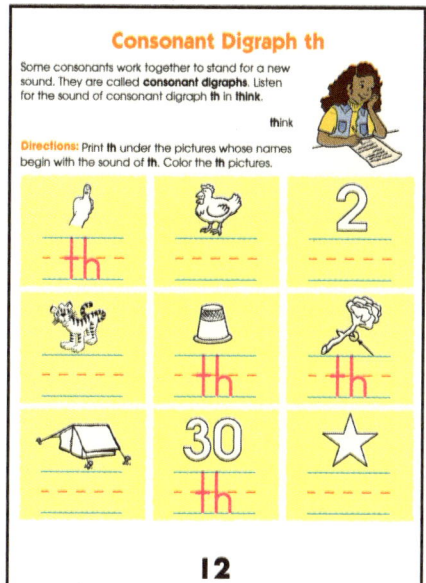

Consonant Digraph th

Some consonants work together to stand for a new sound. They are called **consonant digraphs**. Listen for the sound of consonant digraph **th** in **think**.

think

Directions: Print **th** under the pictures whose names begin with the sound of **th**. Color the **th** pictures.

th		
	th	th
th	th	

12

Read and Write Digraphs

Directions: Write a word from the box to label each picture.

chest   check   sheep
chimp   cherry   thirty
chain   cheese   wheel

cherry	sheep	chain
chest	wheel	cheese
chimp	thirty	check

13

Ending Digraphs

Some words end with consonant digraphs. Listen for the ending digraphs in **duck**, **moth**, **dish**, and **branch**.

duck   moth   dish   branch

Directions: Say the name of each picture. Circle the letters that stand for the ending sound.

(ck) th sh ch	ck (th) sh wh	(ck) th sh ch
ck (th) sh ch	ck th (sh) ch	(ck) th sh ch
ck (th) sh ch	(ck) th sh ch	ck th sh (ch)

14

©2006 School Specialty Publishing   Reading: Grade 2

Missing Digraphs

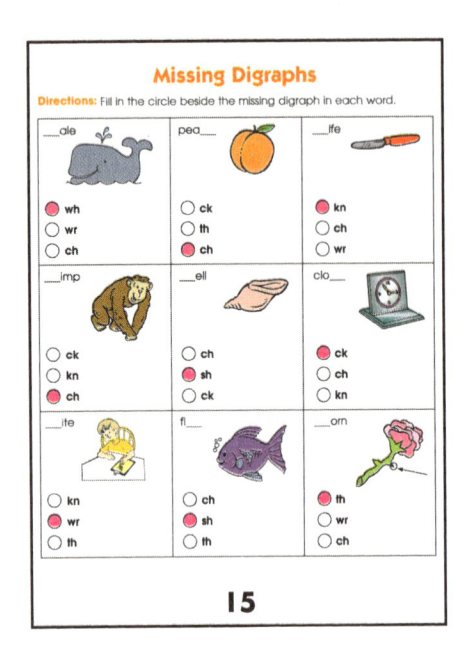

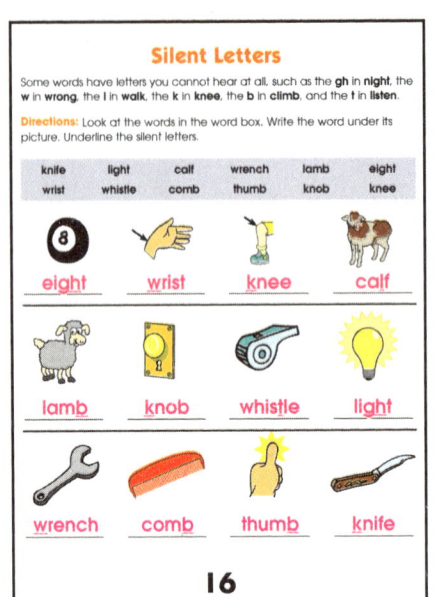

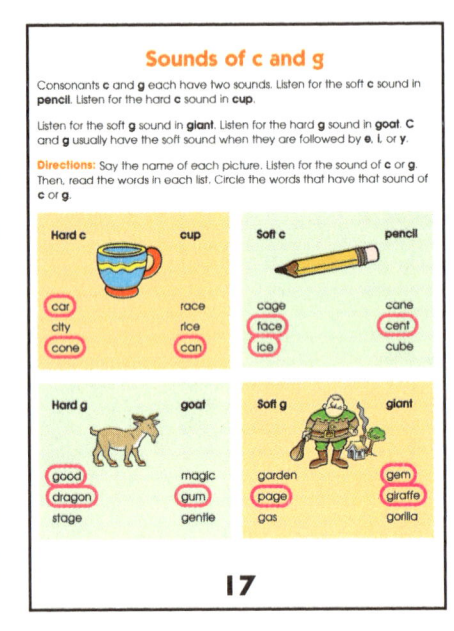

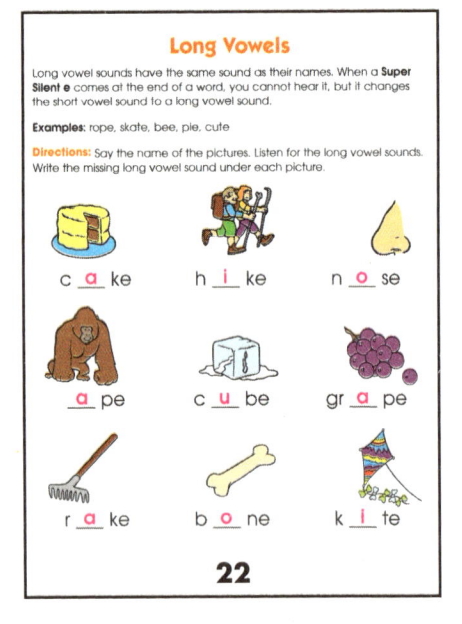

Directions: Fill in the circle beside the missing digraph in each word.

___ale (whale)
● wh
○ wr
○ ch

pea___ (peach)
○ ck
○ th
● ch

___ife (knife)
● kn
○ ch
○ wr

___imp (chimp)
○ ck
○ kn
● ch

___ell (shell)
○ ch
● sh
○ ck

clo___ (clock)
● ck
○ ch
○ kn

___ite (write)
○ kn
● wr
○ th

fi___ (fish)
○ ch
● sh
○ th

___orn (thorn)
● th
○ wr
○ ch

15

Silent Letters

Some words have letters you cannot hear at all, such as the **gh** in **night**, the **w** in **wrong**, the **l** in **walk**, the **k** in **knee**, the **b** in **climb**, and the **t** in **listen**.

Directions: Look at the words in the word box. Write the word under its picture. Underline the silent letters.

| knife | light | calf | wrench | lamb | eight |
| wrist | whistle | comb | thumb | knob | knee |

ei<u>gh</u>t   <u>w</u>rist   <u>kn</u>ee   ca<u>l</u>f

<u>l</u>amb   <u>kn</u>ob   <u>wh</u>istle   li<u>gh</u>t

<u>w</u>rench   com<u>b</u>   thum<u>b</u>   <u>kn</u>ife

16

Sounds of c and g

Consonants **c** and **g** each have two sounds. Listen for the soft c sound in **pencil**. Listen for the hard c sound in **cup**.

Listen for the soft g sound in **giant**. Listen for the hard g sound in **goat**. C and g usually have the soft sound when they are followed by **e**, **i**, or **y**.

Directions: Say the name of each picture. Listen for the sound of **c** or **g**. Then, read the words in each list. Circle the words that have that sound of c or g.

Hard c — cup
(car), race, city, (cone)

Soft c — pencil
cage, cane, (face), (cent), (can), (ice), cube, rice

Hard g — goat
(good), magic, (dragon), (gum), stage, gentle

Soft g — giant
garden, (gem), (page), (giraffe), gas, gorilla

17

Hard and Soft c and g

Directions: Underline the letter that follows the **c** or **g** in each word. Write **hard** if the word has the hard c or hard g sound. Write **soft** if the word has the soft c or soft g sound.

car — hard
wagon — hard
cup — hard

pencil — soft
gym — soft
cot — hard

giant — soft
gem — soft
celery — soft

gum — hard
cymbals — soft
goat — hard

18

Kick It In!

Directions: Write a vowel to complete each word below.

a e i o u

n_e_t

s_o_cks

p_a_ss

r_u_n

k_i_ck

21

Long Vowels

Long vowel sounds have the same sound as their names. When a **Super Silent e** comes at the end of a word, you cannot hear it, but it changes the short vowel sound to a long vowel sound.

Examples: rope, skate, bee, pie, cute

Directions: Say the name of the pictures. Listen for the long vowel sounds. Write the missing long vowel sound under each picture.

c_a_ke   h_i_ke   n_o_se

_a_pe   c_u_be   gr_a_pe

r_a_ke   b_o_ne   k_i_te

22

Reading: Grade 2   72   ©2006 School Specialty Publishing

Super Silent e

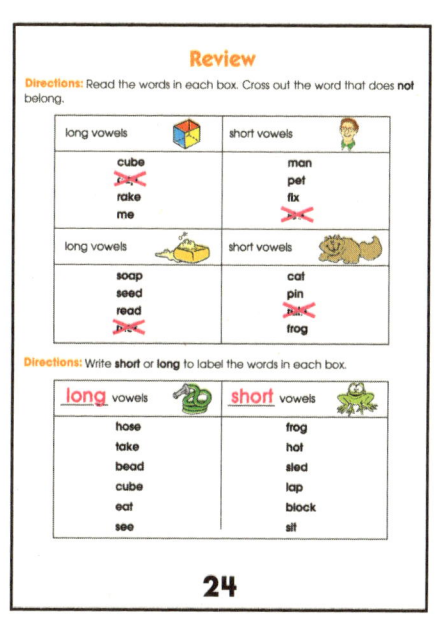

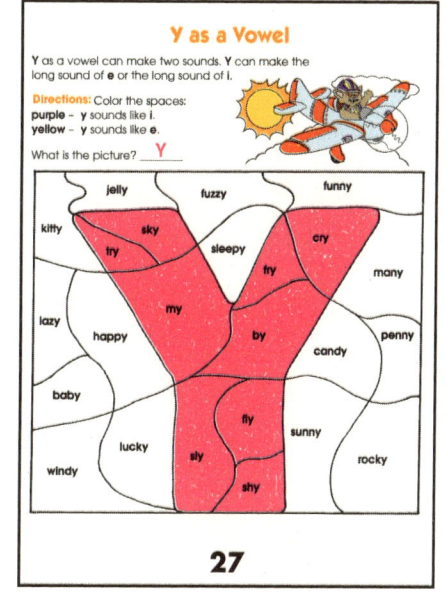

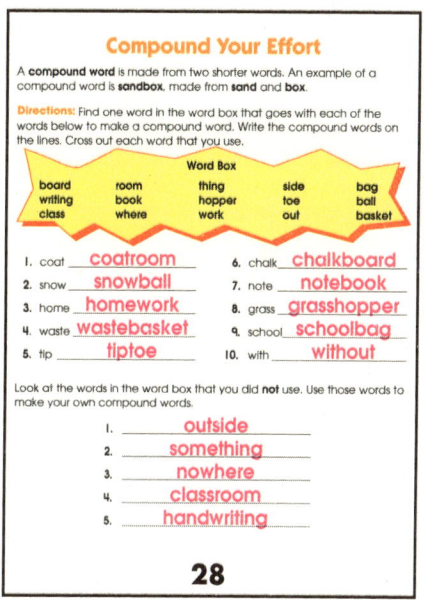

Long vowel sounds have the same sound as their names. When a **Super Silent e** appears at the end of a word, you cannot hear it, but it makes the other vowel have a long sound. For example: **tub** has a **short** vowel sound, and **tube** has a **long** vowel sound.

Directions: Look at the following pictures. Decide if the word has a short or long vowel sound. Circle the correct word. Watch for the **Super Silent e**!

can (cane) tub (tube) rob (robe) rat (rate)
(pin) pine (cap) cape not (note) pan (pane)
slid (slide) dim (dime) tap (tape) cub (cube)

23

Review

Directions: Read the words in each box. Cross out the word that does **not** belong.

long vowels	short vowels
cube	man
~~cat~~	pet
rake	fix
me	~~run~~

long vowels	short vowels
soap	cat
seed	pin
read	~~hut~~
~~red~~	frog

Directions: Write **short** or **long** to label the words in each box.

long vowels	**short** vowels
hose	frog
take	hot
bead	sled
cube	lap
eat	block
see	sit

24

Missing Vowel Pairs

Directions: Fill in the circle beside the missing vowel pair in each word.

t___ ● ie ○ ay ○ oa
tr___ ○ ow ○ ui ● ay
sn___ ● ow ○ ie ○ ay

ch___n ○ ie ○ ui ● ai
gr___ ○ oa ● ay ○ ie
r___d ● oa ○ ay ○ ui

b___ ○ ai ● ow ○ ui
fl___s ● ai ○ oa ○ ie
s___t ● ui ○ ay ○ ie

25

Missing Vowel Pairs

Directions: Fill in the circle beside the missing vowel pair in each word.

h___ ○ ui ○ ow ● ay
tr___n ● oa ○ ai ○ ie
s___p ● oa ○ ai ○ ui

j___ce ○ ai ● ui ○ ie
p___ ○ ui ● oa ○ ie
cr___ ○ ui ○ ay ● ow

g___t ○ ai ● oa ○ ui
fr___t ○ ai ○ ow ● ui
sn___l ○ ow ● ai ○ ie

26

Y as a Vowel

Y as a vowel can make two sounds. **Y** can make the long sound of **e** or the long sound of **i**.

Directions: Color the spaces:
purple – **y** sounds like **i**.
yellow – **y** sounds like **e**.

What is the picture? __Y__

27

Compound Your Effort

A **compound word** is made from two shorter words. An example of a compound word is **sandbox**, made from **sand** and **box**.

Directions: Find one word in the word box that goes with each of the words below to make a compound word. Write the compound words on the lines. Cross out each word that you use.

Word Box
board room thing side bag
writing book hopper toe ball
class where work out basket

1. coat ___coatroom___
2. snow ___snowball___
3. home ___homework___
4. waste ___wastebasket___
5. tip ___tiptoe___
6. chalk ___chalkboard___
7. note ___notebook___
8. grass ___grasshopper___
9. school ___schoolbag___
10. with ___without___

Look at the words in the word box that you did **not** use. Use those words to make your own compound words.

1. ___outside___
2. ___something___
3. ___nowhere___
4. ___classroom___
5. ___handwriting___

28

Mixing a Compound

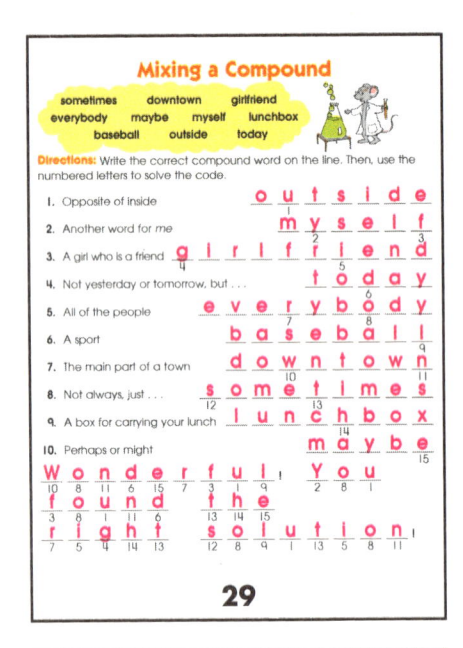

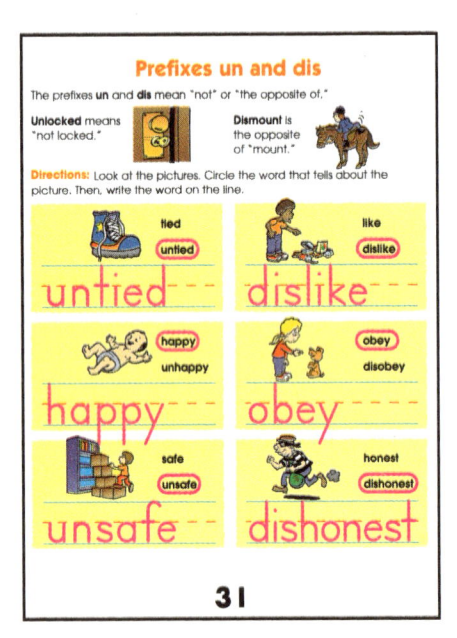

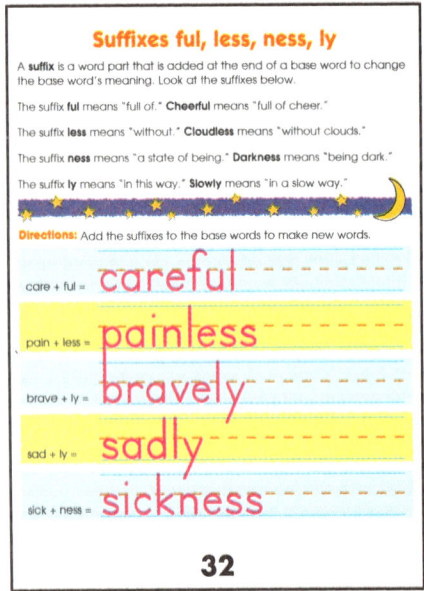

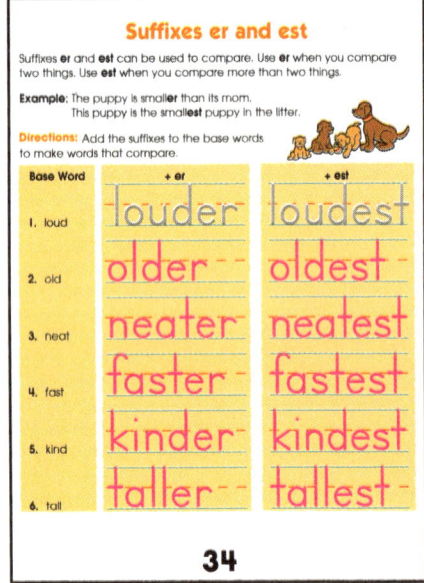

sometimes downtown girlfriend
everybody maybe myself lunchbox
baseball outside today

Directions: Write the correct compound word on the line. Then, use the numbered letters to solve the code.

1. Opposite of inside — o u t s i d e
2. Another word for me — m y s e l f
3. A girl who is a friend — g i r l f r i e n d
4. Not yesterday or tomorrow, but... — t o d a y
5. All of the people — e v e r y b o d y
6. A sport — b a s e b a l l
7. The main part of a town — d o w n t o w n
8. Not always, just... — s o m e t i m e s
9. A box for carrying your lunch — l u n c h b o x
10. Perhaps or might — m a y b e

W o n d e r f u l ! Y o u
f o u n d t h e
r i g h t s o l u t i o n .

29

Prefix re

A **prefix** is a word part. It is added to the beginning of a base word to change the base word's meaning. The prefix **re** means "again."

Example: **Refill** means "to fill again."

Directions: Look at the pictures. Read the base words. Add the prefix **re** to the base word to show that the action is being done again. Write your new word on the line.

read — reread
write — rewrite
paint — repaint
use — reuse
build — rebuild
pay — repay

30

Prefixes un and dis

The prefixes **un** and **dis** mean "not" or "the opposite of."

Unlocked means "not locked."
Dismount is the opposite of "mount."

Directions: Look at the pictures. Circle the word that tells about the picture. Then, write the word on the line.

tied / **untied** — untied
like / **dislike** — dislike
happy / unhappy — happy
obey / disobey — obey
safe / **unsafe** — unsafe
honest / **dishonest** — dishonest

31

Suffixes ful, less, ness, ly

A **suffix** is a word part that is added at the end of a base word to change the base word's meaning. Look at the suffixes below.

The suffix **ful** means "full of." **Cheerful** means "full of cheer."
The suffix **less** means "without." **Cloudless** means "without clouds."
The suffix **ness** means "a state of being." **Darkness** means "being dark."
The suffix **ly** means "in this way." **Slowly** means "in a slow way."

Directions: Add the suffixes to the base words to make new words.

care + ful = careful
pain + less = painless
brave + ly = bravely
sad + ly = sadly
sick + ness = sickness

32

Suffixes and Meanings

Remember: The suffix **ful** means "full of."
The suffix **less** means "without."
The suffix **ness** means "a state of being."
The suffix **ly** means "in this way." The sun shines **brightly**.

Directions: Write the word that matches the meaning.

without pain — painless
in a quick way — quickly
in a neat way — neatly
without fear — fearless
full of grace — graceful
the state of being soft — softness
the state of being sick — sickness
in a glad way — gladly

33

Suffixes er and est

Suffixes **er** and **est** can be used to compare. Use **er** when you compare two things. Use **est** when you compare more than two things.

Example: The puppy is smaller than its mom.
This puppy is the smallest puppy in the litter.

Directions: Add the suffixes to the base words to make words that compare.

Base Word	+ er	+ est
1. loud	louder	loudest
2. old	older	oldest
3. neat	neater	neatest
4. fast	faster	fastest
5. kind	kinder	kindest
6. tall	taller	tallest

34

Reading: Grade 2   74   ©2006 School Specialty Publishing

Scale the Synonym Slope

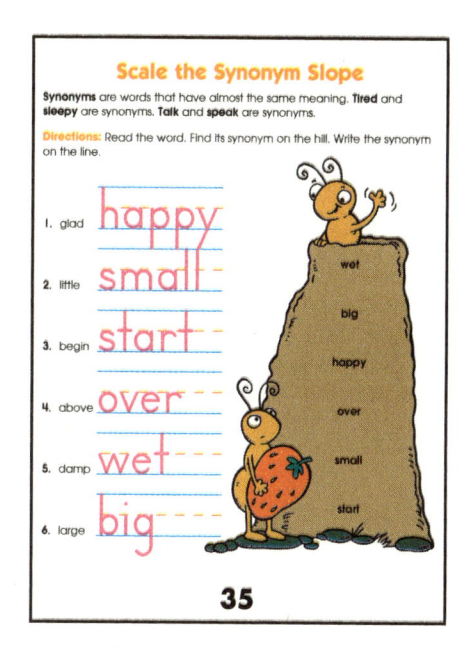

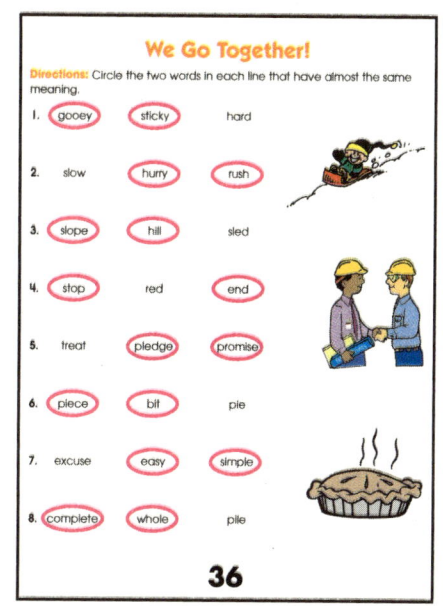

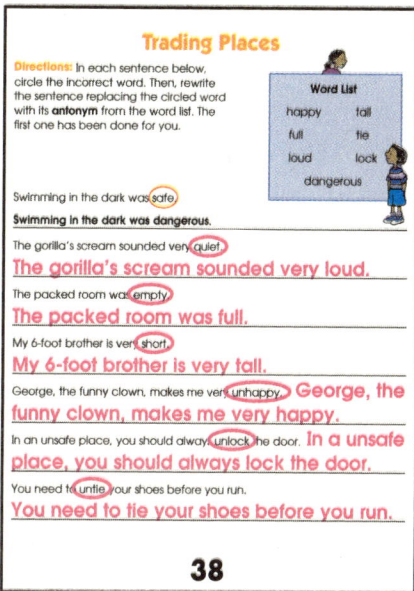

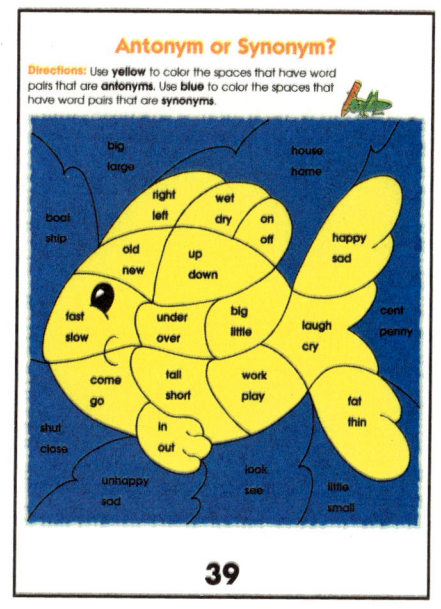

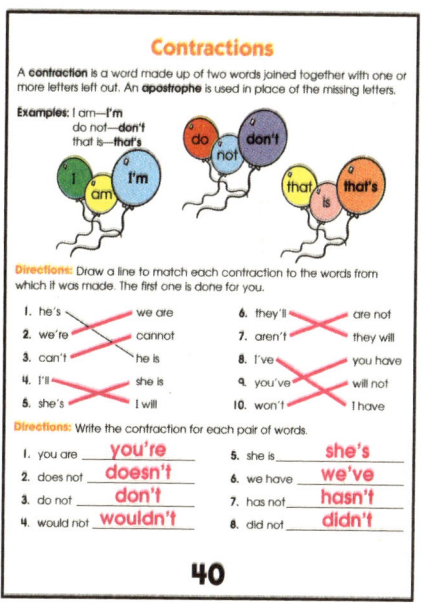

Synonyms are words that have almost the same meaning. **Tired** and **sleepy** are synonyms. **Talk** and **speak** are synonyms.

Directions: Read the word. Find its synonym on the hill. Write the synonym on the line.

1. glad — happy
2. little — small
3. begin — start
4. above — over
5. damp — wet
6. large — big

Hill words: wet, big, happy, over, small, start

We Go Together!

Directions: Circle the two words in each line that have almost the same meaning.

1. (gooey) (sticky) hard
2. slow (hurry) (rush)
3. (slope) (hill) sled
4. (stop) red (end)
5. treat (pledge) (promise)
6. (piece) (bit) pie
7. excuse (easy) (simple)
8. (complete) (whole) pile

Amazing Antonyms

Antonyms are words that have opposite meanings. **Old** and **new** are antonyms. **Laugh** and **cry** are antonyms, too.

Directions: Below each word, write its antonym. Use words from the word box.

Word box: stop, happy, down, go, left, sad, dry

- stop — go
- happy — sad
- right — left
- up — down
- wet — dry

Trading Places

Directions: In each sentence below, circle the incorrect word. Then, rewrite the sentence replacing the circled word with its **antonym** from the word list. The first one has been done for you.

Word List: happy, tall, full, tie, loud, lock, dangerous

Swimming in the dark was (safe).
Swimming in the dark was dangerous.

The gorilla's scream sounded very (quiet).
The gorilla's scream sounded very loud.

The packed room was (empty).
The packed room was full.

My 6-foot brother is very (short).
My 6-foot brother is very tall.

George, the funny clown, makes me very (unhappy).
George, the funny clown, makes me very happy.

In an unsafe place, you should always (unlock) the door.
In a unsafe place, you should always lock the door.

You need to (untie) your shoes before you run.
You need to tie your shoes before you run.

Antonym or Synonym?

Directions: Use **yellow** to color the spaces that have word pairs that are **antonyms**. Use **blue** to color the spaces that have word pairs that are **synonyms**.

Contractions

A **contraction** is a word made up of two words joined together with one or more letters left out. An **apostrophe** is used in place of the missing letters.

Examples: I am—I'm
do not—don't
that is—that's

Directions: Draw a line to match each contraction to the words from which it was made. The first one is done for you.

1. he's — we are
2. we're — cannot
3. can't — he is
4. I'll — she is
5. she's — I will
6. they'll — are not
7. aren't — they will
8. I've — you have
9. you've — will not
10. won't — I have

Directions: Write the contraction for each pair of words.

1. you are — you're
2. does not — doesn't
3. do not — don't
4. would not — wouldn't
5. she is — she's
6. we have — we've
7. has not — hasn't
8. did not — didn't

Proper Nouns

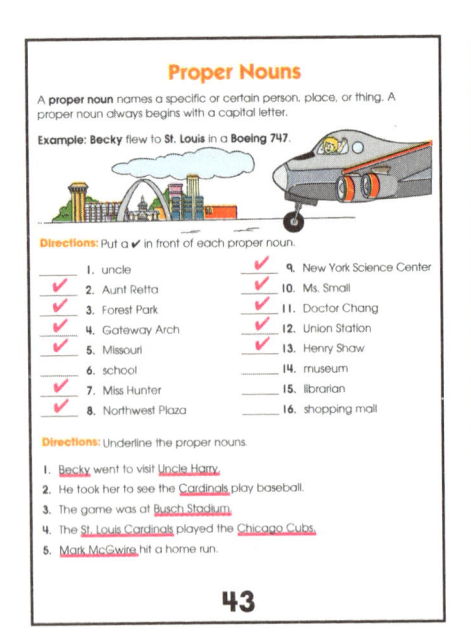

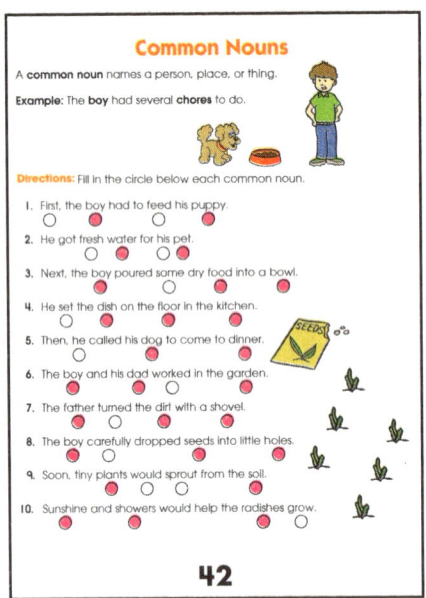

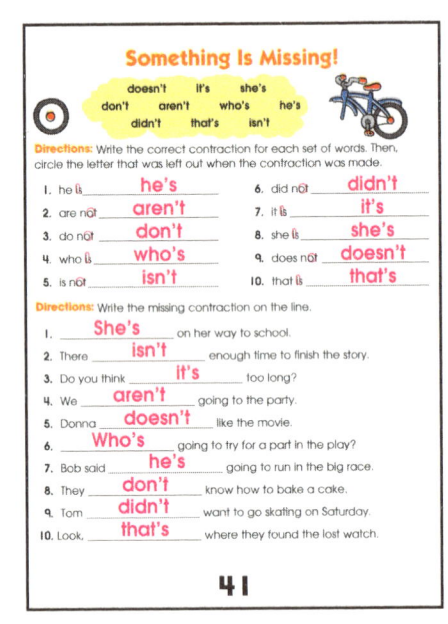

A **proper noun** names a specific or certain person, place, or thing. A proper noun always begins with a capital letter.

Example: **Becky** flew to **St. Louis** in a **Boeing 747**.

Directions: Put a ✔ in front of each proper noun.

___	1. uncle	✔	9. New York Science Center
✔	2. Aunt Retta	✔	10. Ms. Small
✔	3. Forest Park	✔	11. Doctor Chang
✔	4. Gateway Arch	✔	12. Union Station
✔	5. Missouri	✔	13. Henry Shaw
___	6. school	___	14. museum
✔	7. Miss Hunter	___	15. librarian
✔	8. Northwest Plaza	___	16. shopping mall

Directions: Underline the proper nouns.

1. <u>Becky</u> went to visit <u>Uncle Harry</u>.
2. He took her to see the <u>Cardinals</u> play baseball.
3. The game was at <u>Busch Stadium</u>.
4. The <u>St. Louis Cardinals</u> played the <u>Chicago Cubs</u>.
5. <u>Mark McGwire</u> hit a home run.

43

Common Nouns

A **common noun** names a person, place, or thing.

Example: The **boy** had several **chores** to do.

Directions: Fill in the circle below each common noun.

1. First, the **boy** had to feed his **puppy**.
2. He got fresh **water** for his **pet**.
3. Next, the **boy** poured some dry **food** into a **bowl**.
4. He set the **dish** on the **floor** in the **kitchen**.
5. Then, he called his **dog** to come to **dinner**.
6. The **boy** and his **dad** worked in the **garden**.
7. The **father** turned the **dirt** with a **shovel**.
8. The **boy** carefully dropped **seeds** into little **holes**.
9. Soon, tiny **plants** would sprout from the **soil**.
10. **Sunshine** and **showers** would help the **radishes** grow.

42

Something Is Missing!

doesn't   it's   she's
don't   aren't   who's   he's
didn't   that's   isn't

Directions: Write the correct contraction for each set of words. Then, circle the letter that was left out when the contraction was made.

1. he i̶s — **he's**
2. are n̶ot — **aren't**
3. do n̶ot — **don't**
4. who i̶s — **who's**
5. is n̶ot — **isn't**
6. did n̶ot — **didn't**
7. it i̶s — **it's**
8. she i̶s — **she's**
9. does n̶ot — **doesn't**
10. that i̶s — **that's**

Directions: Write the missing contraction on the line.

1. **She's** on her way to school.
2. There **isn't** enough time to finish the story.
3. Do you think **it's** too long?
4. We **aren't** going to the party.
5. Donna **doesn't** like the movie.
6. **Who's** going to try out for a part in the play?
7. Bob said **he's** going to run in the big race.
8. They **don't** know how to bake a cake.
9. Tom **didn't** want to go skating on Saturday.
10. Look, **that's** where they found the lost watch.

41

Singular Nouns

A **singular noun** names one person, place, or thing.

Example: My **mother** unlocked the old **trunk** in the **attic**.

Directions: If the noun is singular, draw a line from it to the trunk. If the noun is not singular, draw an **X** on the word.

teddy bear   hammer   picture   sweater
bonnet   letters ✗   sea shells ✗   fiddle
kite   ring   feather   books ✗
postcard   crayon   doll   dishes ✗
blocks ✗   nails ✗   bicycle   blanket

44

Plural Nouns

A **plural noun** names more than one person, place, or thing.

Example: Some **dinosaurs** ate **plants** in swamps.

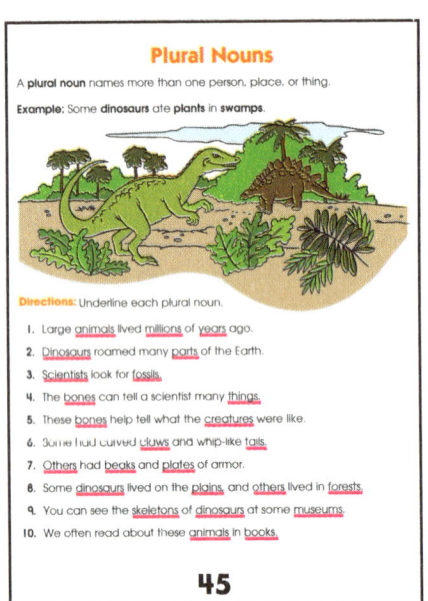

Directions: Underline each plural noun.

1. Large <u>animals</u> lived <u>millions</u> of <u>years</u> ago.
2. <u>Dinosaurs</u> roamed many <u>parts</u> of the Earth.
3. <u>Scientists</u> look for <u>fossils</u>.
4. The <u>bones</u> can tell a scientist many <u>things</u>.
5. These <u>bones</u> help tell what the <u>creatures</u> were like.
6. Some had curved <u>claws</u> and whip-like <u>tails</u>.
7. Others had <u>beaks</u> and <u>plates</u> of armor.
8. Some <u>dinosaurs</u> lived on the <u>plains</u>, and <u>others</u> lived in <u>forests</u>.
9. You can see the <u>skeletons</u> of <u>dinosaurs</u> at some <u>museums</u>.
10. We often read about these <u>animals</u> in <u>books</u>.

45

Action Verbs

A **verb** is a word that can show action.

Example: I **jump**.   He **kicks**.   He **walked**.

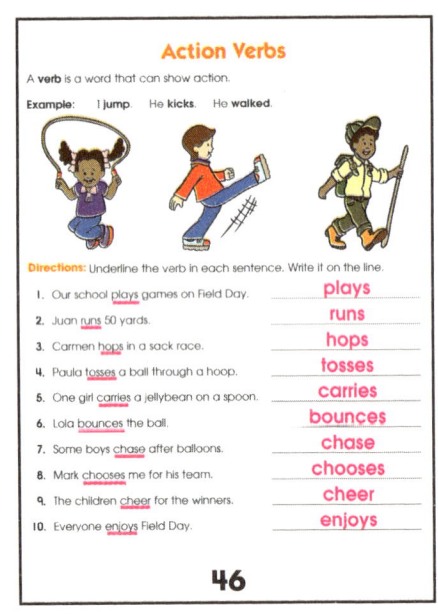

Directions: Underline the verb in each sentence. Write it on the line.

1. Our school <u>plays</u> games on Field Day. — **plays**
2. Juan <u>runs</u> 50 yards. — **runs**
3. Carmen <u>hops</u> in a sack race. — **hops**
4. Paula <u>tosses</u> a ball through a hoop. — **tosses**
5. One girl <u>carries</u> a jellybean on a spoon. — **carries**
6. Lola <u>bounces</u> the ball. — **bounces**
7. Some boys <u>chase</u> after balloons. — **chase**
8. Mark <u>chooses</u> me for his team. — **chooses**
9. The children <u>cheer</u> for the winners. — **cheer**
10. Everyone <u>enjoys</u> Field Day. — **enjoys**

46

Reading: Grade 2   ©2006 School Specialty Publishing

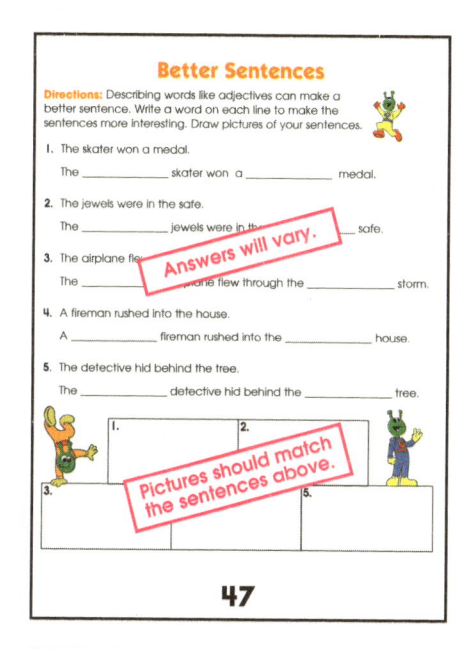

Better Sentences (47)

Directions: Describing words like adjectives can make a better sentence. Write a word on each line to make the sentences more interesting. Draw pictures of your sentences.

1. The skater won a medal.
   The _____ skater won a _____ medal.
2. The jewels were in the safe.
   The _____ jewels were in the _____ safe.
3. The airplane flew through the storm.
   The _____ airplane flew through the _____ storm.
4. A fireman rushed into the house.
   A _____ fireman rushed into the _____ house.
5. The detective hid behind the tree.
   The _____ detective hid behind the _____ tree.

Answers will vary.
Pictures should match the sentences above.

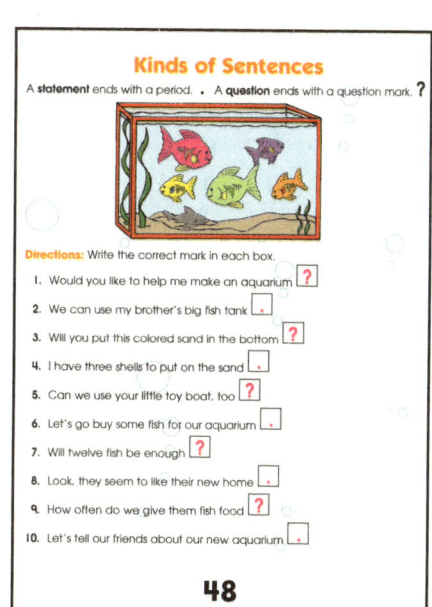

Kinds of Sentences (48)

A **statement** ends with a period. **.** A **question** ends with a question mark. **?**

Directions: Write the correct mark in each box.

1. Would you like to help me make an aquarium [?]
2. We can use my brother's big fish tank [.]
3. Will you put this colored sand in the bottom [?]
4. I have three shells to put on the sand [.]
5. Can we use your little toy boat, too [?]
6. Let's go buy some fish for our aquarium [.]
7. Will twelve fish be enough [?]
8. Look, they seem to like their new home [.]
9. How often do we give them fish food [?]
10. Let's tell our friends about our new aquarium [.]

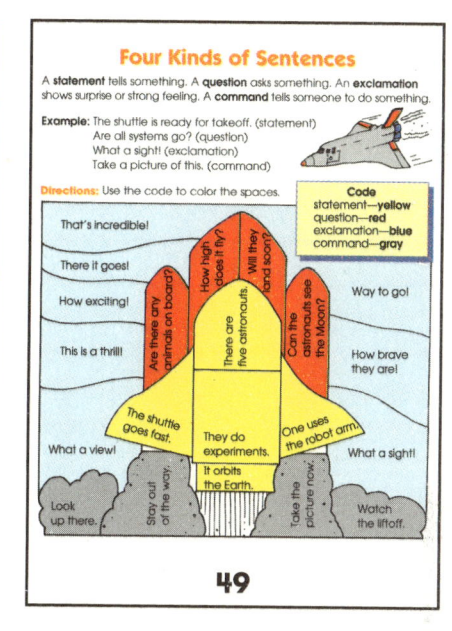

Four Kinds of Sentences (49)

A **statement** tells something. A **question** asks something. An **exclamation** shows surprise or strong feeling. A **command** tells someone to do something.

Example: The shuttle is ready for takeoff. (statement)
Are all systems go? (question)
What a sight! (exclamation)
Take a picture of this. (command)

Directions: Use the code to color the spaces.

Code
statement—yellow
question—red
exclamation—blue
command—gray

That's incredible!
There it goes!
How exciting!
This is a thrill!
What a view!
Look up there.
Stay out of the way.
How high does it fly?
Will they land soon?
Are there any animals on board?
There are five astronauts.
Can the astronauts see the Moon?
The shuttle goes fast.
They do experiments.
It orbits the Earth.
Take the picture now.
One uses the robot arm.
Way to go!
How brave they are!
What a sight!
Watch the liftoff.

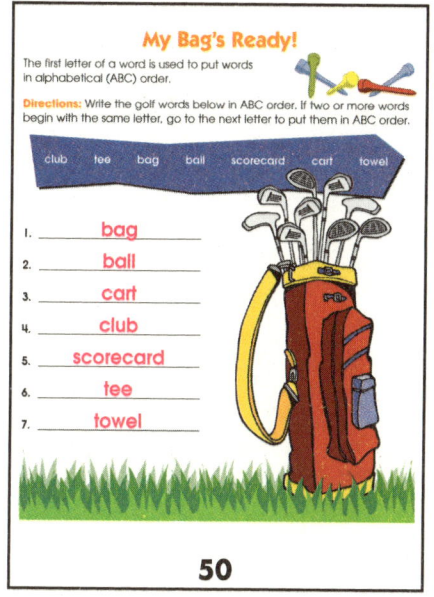

My Bag's Ready! (50)

The first letter of a word is used to put words in alphabetical (ABC) order.

Directions: Write the golf words below in ABC order. If two or more words begin with the same letter, go to the next letter to put them in ABC order.

club   tee   bag   ball   scorecard   cart   towel

1. bag
2. ball
3. cart
4. club
5. scorecard
6. tee
7. towel

Slam Dunk! (51)

Directions: Put the words in the box in ABC order.

coach   points   team   hoop
player   game   score   dunk

1. coach
2. dunk
3. game
4. hoop
5. player
6. points
7. score
8. team

Clue Caper! (52)

Directions: Read the clues below. Write each child's name under the correct picture. Color the hats using the following clues.

Anna   Talia   Sara   Kessia

- Anna is tall and wearing a green top hat. There is a red baseball cap on top of her top hat!
- Sara is short and wearing a blue polka dotted hat.
- Talia has long hair and is standing between Anna and Sara. Talia is wearing a pretty ribbon in her hair with a flower on it.
- Kessia is standing next to Sara. She is wearing a white baker's hat with a purple veil!

How many hats do you count on the page? __4__

Make the Touchdown!

Directions: Read the directions. Draw a line as you move from space to space.

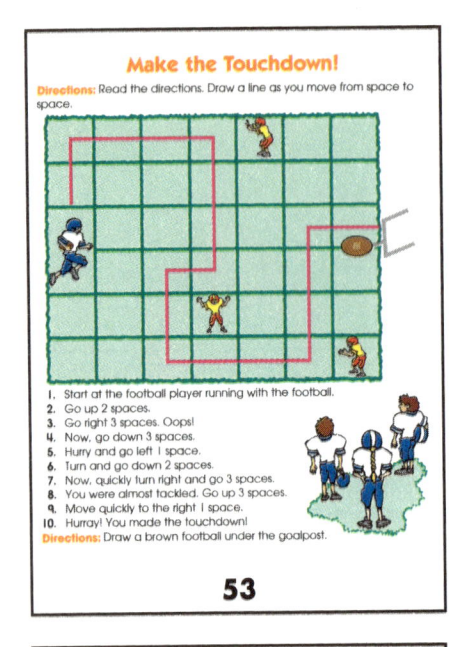

1. Start at the football player running with the football.
2. Go up 2 spaces.
3. Go right 3 spaces. Oops!
4. Now, go down 3 spaces.
5. Hurry and go left 1 space.
6. Turn and go down 2 spaces.
7. Now, quickly turn right and go 3 spaces.
8. You were almost tackled. Go up 3 spaces.
9. Move quickly to the right 1 space.
10. Hurray! You made the touchdown!

Directions: Draw a brown football under the goalpost.

53

Game Story

Directions: Put the basketball story in order. Write the numbers 1–5 on the blanks to show when each event happened.

4 At the end of the regulation game, the score was tied.
1 The teams warmed up before the game.
3 The score at the half was Cougars, 25; Lions, 20.
2 Kim made the first basket of the game.
5 When the overtime ended, the Lions had won the game 50–49.

54

Story Sequence

Look at picture number 4. What do you think happened before Danny went to the amusement park? What might happen when he is at the amusement park?

Directions: You get to decide how the story will go from beginning to end. Write a number in the empty square in each of the other pictures. Choose any number from 1 through 7 (except 4). Number 1 will be what happened first. Number 7 will be what you think happened last.

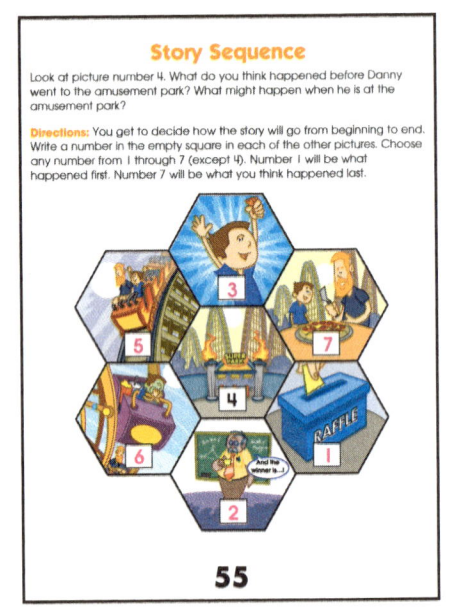

55

Same/Different: Venn Diagram

A **Venn diagram** is a diagram that shows how two things are the same and different.

Directions: Choose two outdoor sports. Then, follow the instructions to complete the Venn diagram.

1. Write the first sport name under the first circle. Write some words that describe the sport. Write them in the first circle.
2. Write the second sport name under the second circle. Write some words that describe the sport. Write them in the second circle.
3. Where the 2 circles overlap, write some words that describe both sports.

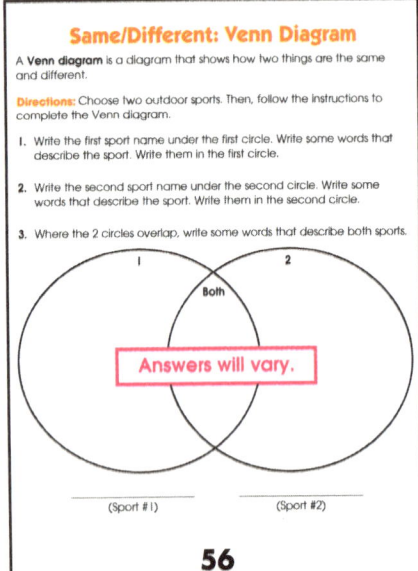

Answers will vary.

(Sport #1)   (Sport #2)

56

Same/Different: Ann and Lee Have Fun

Directions: Read about Ann and Lee. Then, write how they are the same and different in the Venn diagram.

Ann and Lee like to play ball. They like to jump rope. Lee likes to play a card game called "Old Maid." Ann likes to play a card game called "Go Fish."

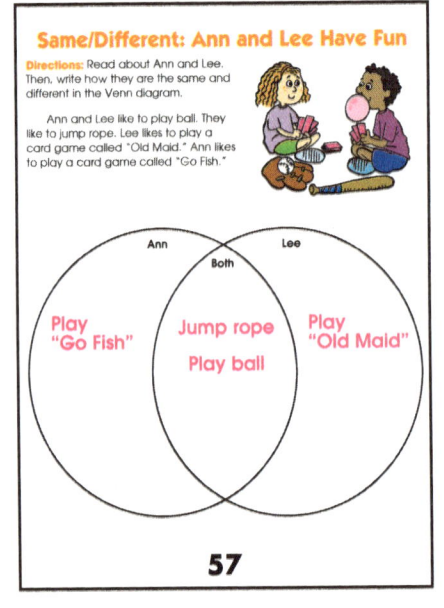

Ann — Play "Go Fish"
Both — Jump rope, Play ball
Lee — Play "Old Maid"

57

Classifying

Sometimes, you want to put things in groups. One way to sort things in groups is to sort them by how they are alike. When you put things together that are alike in some way, you classify them.

You can classify the things in your room. In one group, you can put toys and fun things. In the other group, you can put things that you wear.

Directions: Look at the words on the bedroom door. Put the toys and playthings in the toy box. Put the things you wear in the dresser drawers.

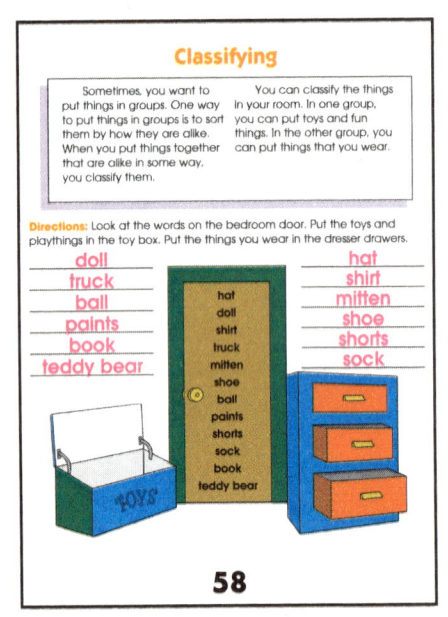

doll
truck
ball
paints
book
teddy bear

hat
shirt
mitten
shoe
shorts
sock

58

Reading: Grade 2   78   ©2006 School Specialty Publishing

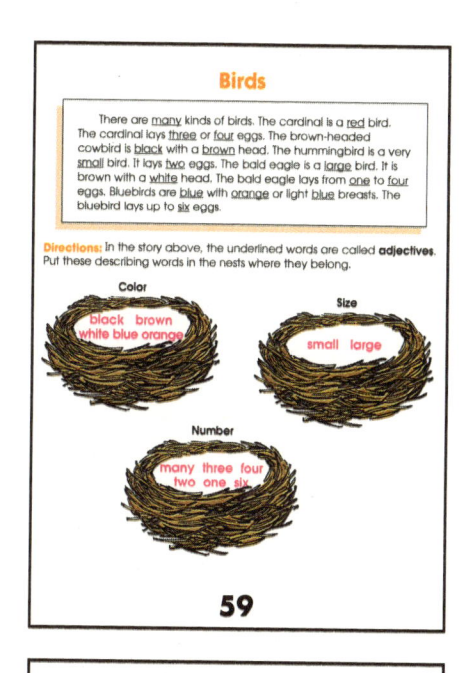

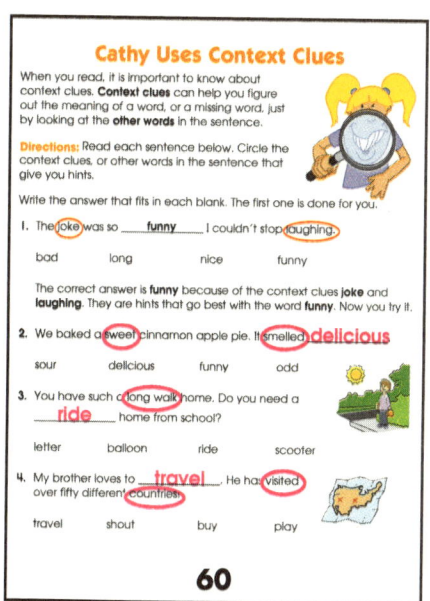

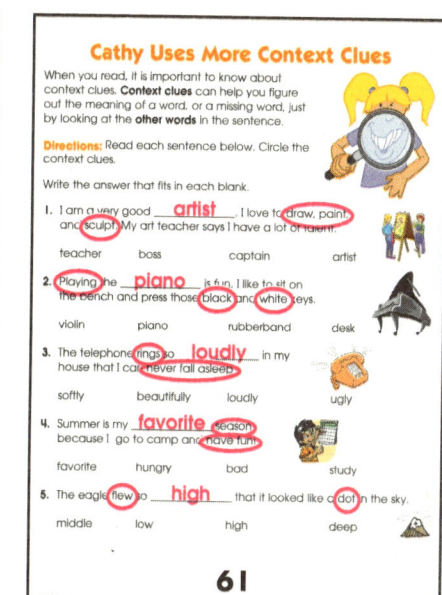

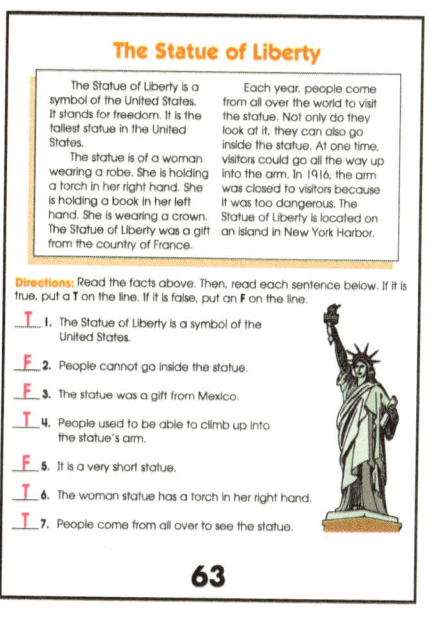

Birds

There are <u>many</u> kinds of birds. The cardinal is a <u>red</u> bird. The cardinal lays <u>three</u> or <u>four</u> eggs. The brown-headed cowbird is <u>black</u> with a <u>brown</u> head. The hummingbird is a very <u>small</u> bird. It lays <u>two</u> eggs. The bald eagle is a <u>large</u> bird. It is brown with a <u>white</u> head. The bald eagle lays from <u>one</u> to <u>four</u> eggs. Bluebirds are <u>blue</u> with <u>orange</u> or light <u>blue</u> breasts. The bluebird lays up to <u>six</u> eggs.

Directions: In the story above, the underlined words are called **adjectives**. Put these describing words in the nests where they belong.

Color: black, brown, white, blue, orange
Size: small, large
Number: many, three, four, two, one, six

Cathy Uses Context Clues

When you read, it is important to know about context clues. **Context clues** can help you figure out the meaning of a word, or a missing word, just by looking at the **other words** in the sentence.

Directions: Read each sentence below. Circle the context clues, or other words in the sentence that give you hints.

Write the answer that fits in each blank. The first one is done for you.

1. The (joke) was so ___funny___ I couldn't stop (laughing).
   bad   long   nice   (funny)

The correct answer is **funny** because of the context clues **joke** and **laughing**. They are hints that go best with the word **funny**. Now you try it.

2. We baked a (sweet) cinnamon apple pie. It (smelled) ___delicious___
   sour   delicious   funny   odd

3. You have such a (long walk) home. Do you need a ___ride___ home from school?
   letter   balloon   ride   scooter

4. My brother loves to ___travel___. He has (visited) over fifty different (countries).
   travel   shout   buy   play

Cathy Uses More Context Clues

When you read, it is important to know about context clues. **Context clues** can help you figure out the meaning of a word, or a missing word, just by looking at the **other words** in the sentence.

Directions: Read each sentence below. Circle the context clues.

Write the answer that fits in each blank.

1. I am a very good ___artist___. I love to (draw), (paint), and (sculpt). My art teacher says I have a lot of talent.
   teacher   boss   captain   artist

2. (Playing) the ___piano___ is fun. I like to sit on the bench and press those (black) and (white) keys.
   violin   piano   rubberband   desk

3. The telephone (rings) so ___loudly___ in my house that I can (never fall asleep).
   softly   beautifully   loudly   ugly

4. Summer is my ___favorite___ (season) because I go to camp and (have fun).
   favorite   hungry   bad   study

5. The eagle (flew) so ___high___ that it looked like a (dot) in the sky.
   middle   low   high   deep

Comprehension: Ladybugs

Directions: Read about ladybugs. Then, answer the questions.

Have you ever seen a ladybug? Ladybugs are red. They have black spots. They have six legs. Ladybugs are pretty!

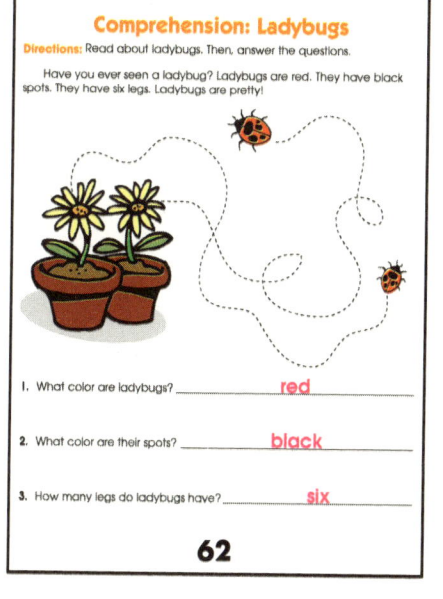

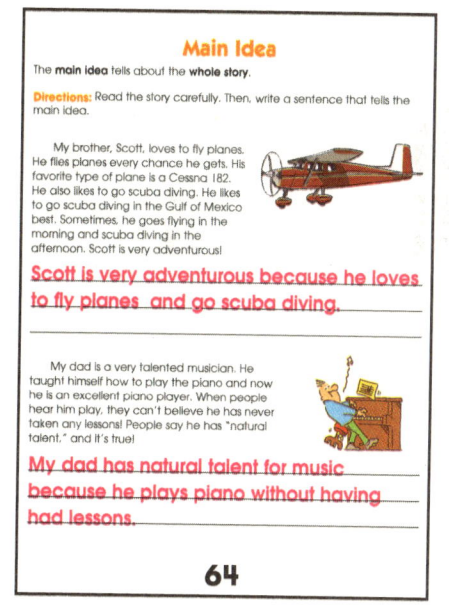

1. What color are ladybugs? ___red___
2. What color are their spots? ___black___
3. How many legs do ladybugs have? ___six___

The Statue of Liberty

The Statue of Liberty is a symbol of the United States. It stands for freedom. It is the tallest statue in the United States.

The statue is of a woman wearing a robe. She is holding a torch in her right hand. She is holding a book in her left hand. She is wearing a crown. The Statue of Liberty was a gift from the country of France.

Each year, people come from all over the world to visit the statue. Not only do they look at it, they can also go inside the statue. At one time, visitors could go all the way up into the arm. In 1916, the arm was closed to visitors because it was too dangerous. The Statue of Liberty is located on an island in New York Harbor.

Directions: Read the facts above. Then, read each sentence below. If it is true, put a **T** on the line. If it is false, put an **F** on the line.

_T_ 1. The Statue of Liberty is a symbol of the United States.
_F_ 2. People cannot go inside the statue.
_F_ 3. The statue was a gift from Mexico.
_T_ 4. People used to be able to climb up into the statue's arm.
_F_ 5. It is a very short statue.
_T_ 6. The woman statue has a torch in her right hand.
_T_ 7. People come from all over to see the statue.

Main Idea

The **main idea** tells about the **whole story**.

Directions: Read the story carefully. Then, write a sentence that tells the main idea.

My brother, Scott, loves to fly planes. He flies planes every chance he gets. His favorite type of plane is a Cessna 182. He also likes to go scuba diving. He likes to go scuba diving in the Gulf of Mexico best. Sometimes, he goes flying in the morning and scuba diving in the afternoon. Scott is very adventurous!

___Scott is very adventurous because he loves to fly planes and go scuba diving.___

My dad is a very talented musician. He taught himself how to play the piano and now he is an excellent piano player. When people hear him play, they can't believe he has never taken any lessons! People say he has "natural talent," and it's true!

___My dad has natural talent for music because he plays piano without having had lessons.___

What Doesn't Belong?

Directions: Read the sentences under each title. Cross out the sentence that does **not** tell about the main idea.

Fun at the Playground
He runs to the slide.
She plays on the swings.
~~I clean my room.~~
They climb the monkey bars.
We sit on the seesaw.

Going to the Zoo
The monkeys climb the trees.
The seals eat fish.
The snakes move slowly.
~~The kitten plays with yarn.~~
The zebra runs fast.

Doing My Homework
I open my book.
~~I take a bath.~~
I read the book.
I write the words.
I add the numbers.

Eating Dinner
Mother cuts the meat.
Father chews the corn.
Sister drinks the milk.
Brother eats his peas.
~~Grandmother has a big house.~~

65

What Will They Do?

Directions: Read each sentence. Fill in the circle beside the best prediction. Then, circle the picture that matches your answer.

The boy is putting on his skates.
○ He will go swimming.
● He will go skating.

The girl fills her glass with milk.
● She will drink the milk.
○ She will drink water.

The woman wrote a letter to her friend.
○ She will call her friend on the phone.
● She will put the letter in the mailbox.

The kids gave Sally a birthday gift.
● She will open the gift.
○ She will throw the gift away.

66

How Will It End?

Directions: Read each story. Fill in the circle beside the sentence that tells what will happen next.

It is a snowy winter night. The lights flicker once, twice, and then they go out. It is cold and dark. Dad finds the flashlight and matches. He brings logs in from outside. What will Dad do?
● Dad will make a fire.
○ Dad will cook dinner.
○ Dad will clean the fireplace.

Maggie has a garden. She likes fresh, homegrown vegetables. She says they make salads taste better. Maggie is going to make a salad for a picnic. What will Maggie do?
○ Maggie will buy the salad at the store.
○ Maggie will buy the vegetables at the store.
● Maggie will use vegetables from her garden.

The big white goose wakes up. It stands and stretches its wings. It looks all around. It feels very hungry. What will the goose do?
○ The goose will go swimming.
● The goose will look for food.
○ The goose will go back to sleep.

67

Clues to Conclusions

Directions: Read each story. Fill in the circle beside the correct conclusion.

Joe tried to read the book. He pulled it closer to his face and squinted. What is wrong?
○ The book isn't very interesting.
● Joe needs glasses.
○ The book is closed.

"My shoes are too tight," said Eddie, "and my pants are too short!" What has happened?
○ Eddie has put on his older brother's clothes.
○ Eddie has become shorter.
● Eddie has grown.

Patsy went to the beach. She stayed outside for hours. When she came home, she looked in the mirror. Her face was very red. Why did she look different?
● Patsy had gotten a bad sunburn.
○ Patsy got red paint all over herself.
○ Patsy was very cold.

68

Extra! Extra! Read All About It!

Newspaper reporters have very important jobs. They have to catch a reader's attention and, at the same time, **tell the facts**.

Newspaper reporters write their stories by answering **who, what, where, when, why,** and **how**.

Directions: Think about a book you just read and answer the questions below.

Who: Who is the story about?
_____

What: What happened to the main character?
_____

Where: Where does _____

When: When does the story take place?
_____

Why: Why do these story events happen?
_____

How: How do these events happen?
_____

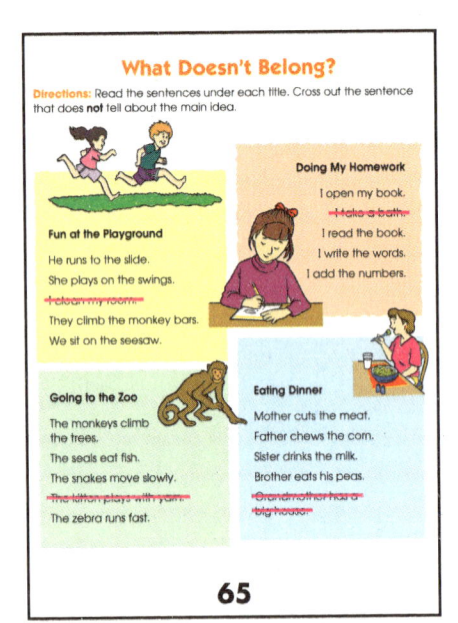

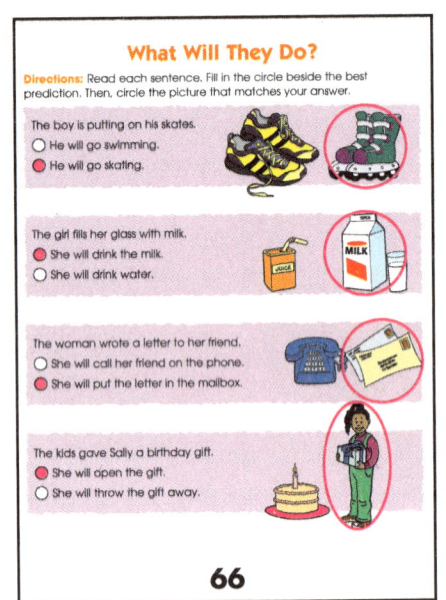

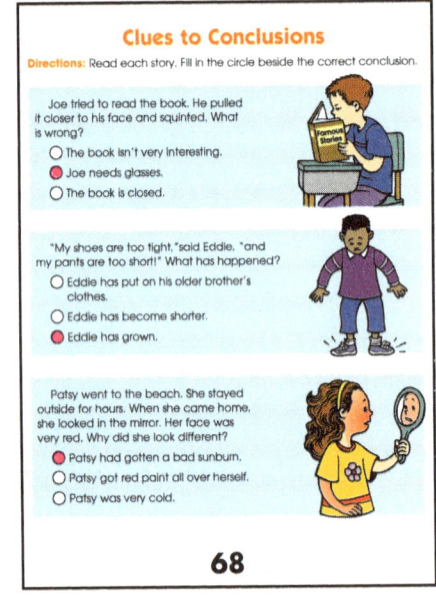

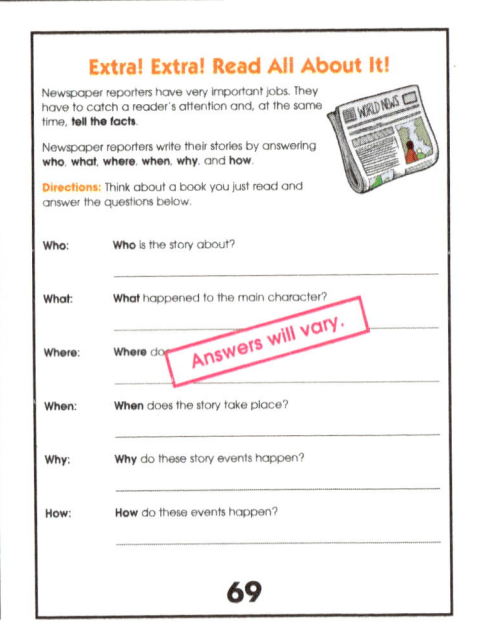

Answers will vary.

69

Reading: Grade 2   80   ©2006 School Specialty Publishing